MW00982213

REAL RESULTS IN A
VIRTUAL ECONOMY
HOW TO FUTURE-PROOF YOUR BUSINESS

DR. DENIS CAUVIER
& SHANE GIBSON

This publication is designed to provide competent and useful information regarding the subject matter covered. However, it is sold with the understanding that the author and publisher are not engaged in rendering legal, financial, or other professional advice. Laws and practices often vary from country to country and province to province. If legal or other expert assistance is required, the services of a professional should be sought. The author and the publisher specifically disclaim any liability that is incurred from the use or application of the contents of this book. First Edition, First Printing – Copyright © 2021 by DAX Enterprises International Inc. All rights reserved under International and Pan-American Copyright Conventions. No part of this book may be reproduced in any form or by any means, electronic or mechanical, including photocopying without permission in writing from the publisher. All inquiries should be addressed to DAX Enterprises International Inc.

Special Technical Contributor Julian Lee
Cover design by Debraj Dey
Edited by Masumi Parmar
Layout by Dr. Jay Polmar
Back cover photo by Martin Spicer
Printed in Canada by RR Donnelley Inc. 10 9 8 7 6 5 4 3 2 1
ISBN 978-0-9736514-9-2

OTHER BOOKS BY DR. DENIS CAUVIER:

- How to Hire the Right Person
- How to Keep Your Staff Productive & Happy
- Achieve It! A Personal Success Journal
- The ABC's of Making Money (co-authored with Alan Lysaght)
- Attracting, Selecting and Retaining GREAT People
- The ABC's of Making Money 4 Teens (co-authored with Alan Lysaght)
- 101 Low Cost/High Impact Recruiting Methods
- Hired 2.0 Recruiting Exceptional Talent at the Speed of Light
- Getting Rich – How to Avoid Being Ripped Off … (co-authored with Alan Lysaght)
- You're HIRED – How to Land Your Dream Job
- Financial Freedom – How to Profit from Your Perfect Business (co-authored with Alan Lysaght)
- The Art & Science of Making Money
- Strategic Talent Management – How to Boost Your Profits in a Disruptive Economy
- Bullet Proof – Mental Toughness the Key to Winning in Life

OTHER BOOKS BY SHANE GIBSON

- Closing Bigger – The Field Guide to Closing Bigger Deals (co-authored with Captain Trevor Greene)
- Sociable! How Social Media is Turning Sales and Marketing Up-side Down (co-authored with Stephen Jagger)
- Guerilla Social Media Marketing – 100+ Weapons to Grow Your Online Influence, Attract Customers, and Drive Profits (co-authored with Jay Conrad Levinson)

CONTENTS

INTRODUCTION

"The world has gone through two years' worth of
digital transformation in two months."

- SATYA NADELLA, MICROSOFT CEO, APRIL 2020

Everything changed. Employees were sent out of the office to work from home. People were asked to physically distance and socialize digitally. Children attended online classes. Most forms of sports and entertainment were shut down. Customers got used to ordering online and having things delivered. These abrupt yet supposedly "temporary" changes in the way people live, work, and consume products and services have now become permanent shifts in the marketplace.

While industry leaders have proactively chosen to become digital-first enterprises, many are struggling to navigate this new virtual economy. Some companies were steamrolled and became irrelevant overnight. What about you? Can you lead your organization through rapid changes and trends such as the rise of remote workers and remote customers?

The great news is that the technologies needed to future-proof your business already exist. They are proven, tested, user friendly, and affordable, even for SMEs. The *real* challenge is the cultural change required to adopt a digital-first mindset. To be successful in this new economy, you need two things: 1) a digital-first customer-centric sales strategy and 2) an agile and tech-literate organizational culture to support #1.

Elon Musk is an example of a digital-first thinker whose company, Tesla, is a digital-first market disruptor. When he built and grew the company, he focused on truly building a technology platform that enabled automobiles. They are literally computers on wheels, not cars with computers in them.

Stage Kings of Sydney, Australia is a fascinating example of a company that rapidly embraced that digital-first mindset and won. For a decade, its business model had been based upon creating very large, complex, customized stages for concerts, special corporate events, and athletic competitions. It built stages for Miley Cyrus, the Melbourne Music Festival, and the opening ceremony stage for the 2018 Commonwealth Games. These were huge corporate contracts. When the work-from-home rules were enacted by the Australian government, their business model collapsed overnight. An entire year of contracts was immediately canceled.

Instead of sulking, the company decided to focus its energy on the new norm and use its design, project management, and carpentry skills differently. People are working from home, so they came up with the idea of the IsoKing Desk. They understood that virtual workers needed a small yet practical, attractive, and affordable desk, and they needed them right away. They quickly came up with a great concept and offered it to their small following on social media. The design resonated with people and the orders started coming in. Satisfied customers began to share product pictures and reviews online with their networks. Within several weeks, the local media were interviewing the founders as an example of local ingenuity and resilience during the crisis. This generated even more attention, which led to more sales and coverage from hundreds of media outlets around the world.

From then on, the company rebranded itself as IsoKings and decided to invest heavily in an ecommerce site. It engaged its growing community and gathered feedback about the home wood products they would be interested in. The ideas came fast and furious, from stand-up desks and storage solutions to wooden wine racks. The company tested the waters to see which of these ideas got traction. The best ideas were then offered on individual GoFundMe campaigns. To date, over 40 new products have been successfully launched this way. The company is profitable and fully digital. Not only did all original employees retain their jobs, but IsoKings had to hire more workers, and is poised for growth.

This is just one of the many success stories of organizations around the globe that have become prosperous digital-first enterprises during a time of crisis. These were not accidental strokes of luck. It requires a specific mindset and specific tools to achieve this kind of success.

You have an opportunity to re-evaluate (and possibly reset) your business model, culture, and values to not just adapt but thrive in this new virtual economy.

This book has been written to provide you with a logical, strategic approach to become a digital-first enterprise. As such, you can:

- Eliminate intermediaries and gain direct access to customers, employees, and the community.
- Have a direct positive influence on your brand and the conversations about it.
- Greatly reduce (and even eliminate) traditional expenditures such as travel and commercial leasing.
- Reduce your carbon footprint and environmental impact.
- Create more business opportunities by putting your brand and sales team right where the customer is — on digital platforms, networks, and channels.
- Become more responsive and resilient. With fewer fixed costs, legacy systems, and a more adaptable culture, new challenges, and market changes can become springboards instead of roadblocks.

Of course, with a wide range of business verticals and industries, the topics to be discussed could bloat up a book into 5,000 pages. Using the Pareto Principle, we decided to focus on the 20% of the possible actions you could take that are going to get you 80% of the results.

Based upon our collective 50+ years of experience working with high-performing teams, we will tackle four areas to get you the furthest fastest in your digital transformation:

1. What a digital-first enterprise is and what it takes to become one.

2. How to attract, select, hire, onboard, train, develop, lead, and engage virtual teams.

3. How to leverage digital and social selling tools to become highly competitive in the marketplace.

4. How to establish yourself as a thought leader and your company as a recognized digital brand in your target markets.

Whether you're a Fortune 500 CEO or a one-person show, whether you're manufacturer, professional service organization, tech company, non-profit, government, or a small business, the principles in this book will help you thrive in this virtual economy.

Let's get started.

CHAPTER 1

DIGITAL-FIRST: WHAT IS IT, REALLY?

*"[the present crisis] is accelerating the growth
of e-commerce, bringing changes that
were expected in 2030 to today's market."*

- TOBI LUTKE THE CEO OF SHOPIFY

The news is encouraging: evidence shows that a business's bottom line can be improved by embracing a digital-first strategy. It is abundantly clear to anyone who doesn't live in a cave that organizations which have failed to shift to a digital-first strategy have suffered for it. The list of companies that have closed or been damaged severely is overwhelming, and quite frankly too negative to put in our positive book. Conversely organizations that were digital-first prior to the pandemic not only survived but thrived.

There are many financial benefits of remote teams, discussed in detail later in the book. Some of the ROIs realised include: higher levels of productivity, lower real estate costs, greater employee engagement and more client loyalty.

One of the biggest opportunities in this new virtual economy is that you can now market, sell and distribute almost anything globally. With tools like Amazon, Alibaba and networks like LinkedIn and Facebook you can connect with and market to anyone. This provides a massive opportunity to scale your business efficiently and profitably. Conversely, the bad news is that someone from across the globe is now targeting customers in your backyard. You have to start looking at your business through a global and multicultural ecommerce lens.

*[global selling stat] "96 percent of all of the world's consumers
and over three-quarters of the world's purchasing power
are outside of the United States"*

- LINDA MCMAHON, HEAD OF THE U.S. SMALL BUSINESS ADMINISTRATION

Post Covid-19 the world will not abandon the virtual economy; it is here to stay. Yes, some people will go back to offices, and large in-person meetings will happen again, but organizations have clearly seen the benefits of virtual. They will continue to do business virtually, even if in some cases via a hybrid model. We believe that the offices of the future will be small centers focusing on connections, excellence and collaboration, where in in-person workshops, brainstorming sessions and meetings will happen with teammates, clients and other stakeholders. Large-screen monitors will be installed in common areas, allowing workers to share a virtual coffee with friends working from home. Companies that want to thrive and obtain real results in the digital age will need to master the principles, strategies, and tech tools covered in this book.

DID YOU KNOW?

A survey from Gartner HR reveals that 88% of organizations across the globe have encouraged or required employees to work from home during the crisis. Gartner research also shows that 74% intend to shift some employees to remote work permanently.

Consumers and business decisions makers are now digital-first and mobile-first. Their methods of discovering, researching and engaging brands and suppliers often start on mobile phones. As industry leaders our business model, marketing, human resource strategy, sales process and customer experience must all put the online experience first. A digital-first strategy is a customer-centric strategy because your customers are now digital-first. Digital is not *how* we do things; it's *why* we do things.

> *"It doesn't matter if you want to send your sales team out to visit clients in-person, if your customers prefer to meet with them virtually."*
>
> - SHANE GIBSON

There is a lot of buzz surrounding the notion of digital-first. Before going any further, let us define what it is, in the context used in this book.

Digital-first is a mindset that involves the culture, structures, and processes that support digital optimization. Many people mistakenly think that it's solely about using technology for the sake of using technology. Giving all employees new smartphones loaded with the latest apps is a digital *tactic*, yes; but it's not a digital-first solution unless it is part of a comprehensive strategy. This strategy has to start with a digital-first culture that is aligned with the mission, vision, and core values of the business.

A digital-first culture creates an environment that shows all personnel the merits of digital-first, and then supports people in digital fluency and core competency through training and development. To reinforce this culture, organizations can structure themselves less formally to improve effectiveness and agility. They can provide collaboration tools that encourage and support virtual teamwork. Organizations can design and implement new, more digitally fluid, and flexible processes, such as new employee onboarding and management systems that provide dynamic feedback.

Almost every industry has been impacted by external factors forcing them to connect with customers and teammates digitally. The key is to not assume a victim mindset; rather, recognize that this is a once-in-a-generation opportunity. This is a springboard, not an obstacle!

Everyone needs to be digitally literate, but it's the humanity in our organizations that will be the true differentiator. You cannot out-tech or outspend a monolith like Amazon, but you *can* bring more value to the marketplace by integrating tech with authentic engagement strategies in everything, from hiring to managing personalized relationships with clients.

Just telling your team to "go virtual" isn't enough. You must create a flexible remote or in-and-out-of-office hybrid. It's about *asking* your team what formats and even functional work hours look like. Productivity and balance are not one-size-fits-all. Ultimately, you want to provide your team the technology platforms, tools, and guidelines, then let them build the balanced model that works for them. In the most agile organizations, you'll see staff at all levels and leadership actively coming together and developing playbooks to manage this new work reality.

> **Everyone needs to be digitally literate, but it's the humanity in our organizations that will be the true differentiator. You cannot out-tech or outspend a monolith like Amazon, but you can bring more value to the marketplace by integrating tech with authentic engagement strategies in everything, from hiring to managing personalized relationships with clients.**

"If you don't measure the right things, you can't get an accurate picture of where you are, what your blind spots are or how you can improve."

- DR. DENIS CAUVIER

One of the first steps in managing this new frontier is assessing your digital readiness.

It is critical to know where you are (current assets and capabilities) and where you want to go. Once you have collected your data, you can begin navigating your path to digital success.

DIGITAL-FIRST ENTERPRISE READINESS ASSESSMENT

For each statement, rate your organization on a scale of 1-5 where:
1 = Strongly disagree 2 = Disagree 3 = Neutral 4 = Agree 5 = Strongly agree

Statement	1	2	3	4	5
Our mission and vision statements reflect a customer-centric, digital-first perspective.					
The entire organization is aware of and committed to delivering our mission and vision.					
Each staff has a sense of purpose that is strongly linked to their job.					
Our organization achieves our strategic objectives.					
Our organization sets, communicates, and measures enterprise-wide digital KPIs.					
Our organization routinely meets or exceeds enterprise-wide digital KPIs.					
Our organization recognizes and rewards teams that meet or exceed digital KPIs.					
Our business strategy is shared and understood at all levels of the organization.					
Our brand is positively perceived on all relevant digital channels.					
Our brand has the highest profile in our industry.					
Our brand is perceived as excellent in quality and value of products, services, and client service.					
Our brand ranks high on eco-awareness, fair trade practices, employee relations, and commitment to diversity.					
Our organization recognizes and rewards innovation and new ideas.					
Our organization implements and manages change well.					
Previous change initiatives in our organization have been successful.					
Our organization embraces the assessment and application of new technology.					
Our business strategy integrates digital products and services.					
Our organization evaluates and adopts new ways of working (e.g., Agile, Lean).					
Our organization has a leader who is in charge of and accountable for digital initiatives.					
Our organization has senior managers outside of IT who are involved in defining, designing, and implementing digital initiatives.					
Opportunities to automate business processes are identified, assessed, and implemented where appropriate.					
Past technology implementations in our organization have been successful.					

Statement	1	2	3	4	5
Our organization uses technologies such as AI, VR, Big Data, and Robotics.					
Our remote teams function well and regularly achieve intended targets/outcomes.					
Our organization has stable, partnership-based supplier relationships.					
Our supply chain is fully digital.					
Our organization has a stable workforce with low staff turnover.					
Our organization has an open, collaborative culture.					
Our organization communicates effectively internally and externally.					
Our employees understand their roles and responsibilities.					
Our employees understand and follow defined processes and procedures.					
Our organization fosters continuous learning and professional development.					
Our employees have autonomy and ownership.					
Our company does an excellent job at ecommerce.					
Our company has a comprehensive social and digital selling strategy.					
Our sales team consistently executes the social and digital sales strategy effectively.					
Our company uses digital tools to maximize customer success.					
Our company uses digital tools to maximize customer experience.					

Understanding your score:

There is a correlation between your scores and your company's readiness for digital reinvention. Consistently scoring 1 or 2 means that you are not yet ready to embrace and capitalize on your digital reinvention journey. Scoring 4 and 5 on the above elements means you have a solid foundation for a successful, sustained digital reinvention.

THE 5 STAGES OF DIGITAL REINVENTION

We like to use the term "Digital Reinvention" instead of "Digital Maturity." Maturity makes it sound like we have *arrived* as an organization. Words like "legacy," "established" and "aging" go along with the term. Reinvention, on the other hand, is about proactively reaching forward into the future, and having a culture of innovation and evolution. You must keep your culture, technology, brand and sales process evolving, constantly reinventing your organization to stay relevant.

Dynamic, turbulent marketplaces require reinvention. That environment has been the norm for far longer than any recent crisis, and it's high time organizations caught up.

North American and European business culture have far greater resistance to change than many emerging markets. Companies tend to defend the status quo from a business process and technology perspective. When you look at markets like Asia or Africa the resistance to reinvention is less because consumers and business leaders are used to coping with uncertainty and rapidly shifting economic landscapes. China, with its rapid growth, has moved through a period of rapid change where entire cities with millions of citizens have materialized out of rural farmland in a period of 10-20 years. In that same period, they industrialized and then digitized their economy, in many cases leapfrogging other countries.

In the past two decades, developed nations have had marginal population growth and comparatively steady but slow economic growth. Established economic leaders have used technology to prop up old processes and business models, but haven't really reinvented their organizations. As we hesitated to embrace technology, our competitors have gotten a big head start. That said, the powerful thing about technology is that if you embrace the new and are willing to reinvent yourself, you, too, can leapfrog around the competition to embrace opportunity.

Our path to digital reinvention should include evaluating existing disruptive technologies, assessing how they can future-proof our business and determining how we can integrate them into our enterprise. Some of the top disruptive technologies today that you may want to evaluate include:

- IoT (the Internet of Things)
- AI (Artificial Intelligence)
- VR/AR (Virtual and Augmented Reality)
- Blockchain
- 4D Printing
- Autonomous Vehicles
- Smart Dust
- Brain-computer Interfaces
- Natural Language Question Answering
- Smart Robots
- Commercial UAVs (Drones)
- Connected Homes
- Virtual Personal Assistants
- Voice Search

It's important to note that this list will have changed within months of publishing this book. It's vital that we look to forward thinking research organizations such as Gartner or Deloitte to stay up to date with the latest disruptive tech innovations.

One Alberta-based oil company realized huge gains from digitizing an analogue business process. An oil company obviously can't make their oil wells or extraction 100% virtual or digital. However, there are still many remote monitoring and work components that save time, resources and money. Leveraging digital tools they realized a reduced cost of extraction per barrel by more than 30%.

They use remote monitoring sensors (IoT) connected to a Salesforce.com app back at operations. When a storage tank is about to become full, headquarters is automatically alerted. Previously this would force a stop in production if drivers did not come empty the tank promptly. In addition to this, drivers would often show up, only to discover that a well's storage tank was not even close to full. This often resulted in paying shipping costs for a full tanker when it was really half-empty. When the company automated and remotely monitored tank levels, they greatly reduced their costs for extraction, while production simultaneously increased because of improved capacity. The scheduling and alerts were all driven by SalesForce.com instead of humans and paper notations used previously. This is not an isolated story as comparably impressive gains are being realized in agriculture, manufacturing, and distribution industries, just to name a few. Pairing IoT with machine learning and platforms like SalesForce.com can drive massive efficiencies in traditional industries.

The unstoppable march of technology and the change it catalyzes make many feel more victimized than empowered by it. We work with many organizations, helping them embrace digital sales and HR shifts, and the attitudes we encounter there have been eye opening. Staff often see technology changes as intrusions on their turf. It can seem to them like senior management is paid to invent new ways to disrupt things that are "working just fine." As with any strategic change, a digital reinvention must start and be driven from the top. Although it's very important to have the support of HR and IT departments, this change can't be soley lead by them.

This quote sums up a stark reality that you can miss when focused on the microcosm of your individual role:

> "If the rate of change on the outside exceeds
> the rate of change on the inside, the end is near."
>
> – JACK WELCH

Contrary to the impression, senior management is *not* actually sitting around inventing new ways to use technology changes to disrupt staff. What they're really doing is responding appropriately to rapidly changing outside forces. Your ability to implement these changes to rapidly depends on your company's stage of reinvention. Ad hoc or reactive cultures struggle, whereas proactive and systematic reinventors tend to lead the change and reap the largest rewards.

THE 5 STAGES OF DIGITAL REINVENTION:

STAGE 1 – RESISTANT

This stage is often referred to as the status quo stage. Here, an organization is well-established and invested in its business processes. It has legacy HR, marketing, sales, and logistics approaches that it has established over time. In many cases, it has invested heavily in old tech or even invested in avoiding the use of tech, if possible. The drive to change or adapt to new technology or new market approaches usually comes too late, too little, and often out of desperation to survive. IT is a small department or fully outsourced and their overall tech savviness is moderate or outdated. Such an organization doesn't invest in gathering intelligence, insights, or expertise in emerging technologies and market trends.

From a customer engagement perspective, customers have to adhere to the company's method of doing business to access products and services. This rigidity in business process and technology adoption makes it difficult to respond to external threats, market changes, and opportunities.

STAGE 2 – REACTIVE

Reactive organizations are grudgingly open to technology changes and market shifts, but they tend to lack the processes, people, and insights to capitalize on them in a timely or efficient manner. One business owner of a pub and hotel group in Vancouver summarized it well when he said, "We are so busy making the money we are making, we are not thinking strategically about the money we're not making." He knew they should be heavily investing in social media marketing and digital platforms, but his pub and restaurant were already booming and understaffed.

These organizations tend to copy what their competitors are doing or react to what their customers request. The stimulus is usually in the form of a customer complaint or watching a new competitor mop up market share. Their attitude toward tech tends to be positive, but their decisions aren't strategic. They see it as a tactic or a tool rather than an organizational value. It's something applied in pockets of the business with very little process, inter-departmental collaboration, or accountability. Many staff don't see themselves as tech people and are happy to use it as little as possible. A lot of tech initiatives are implemented with a hands-off approach, i.e., a small group of people is empowered to make tech decisions and investments. This group tends to operate in a bubble and may not have the business process knowledge or business acumen that would help implement the technology in the right context. Because of this, they may not select or even understand how to find best-of-breed technology tools and platforms. In a sales organization it could also mean that only a select group of self-motivated salespeople are using tech tools like CRM or LinkedIn Sales Navigator and reaping the benefits, while the sales organization as a whole is lagging.

STAGE 3 – RESPONSIVE

Responsive organizations are much like reactive ones, at first glance. They tend to play catch-up with competitors and customer demands. What gives them an advantage is they are more strategic and formalized in their approach. It's about seeing the big picture and seeing how technology can help you in the immediate future. This responsiveness is customer centric. It is more connected with what is currently becoming popular in the marketplace or what their competitors have recently implemented.

These organizations don't tend to be digital-first, but they realize returns on technology by using it to enhance or augment existing business practices.

They invest in a tool not because someone else is using it, but because there's a business case for it. Responsive organizations tend to be more collaborative and technology initiatives tend to involve multiple departments. They may even use outside experts to evaluate technology solutions along with developing digital sales and marketing strategies.

One of the challenges at this stage is it's still a game of catch-up. It's about strategically keeping up with what is already being broadly used in the marketplace. This strategy will keep you relevant but won't give you a major competitive advantage.

STAGE 4 – PROACTIVE

The proactive stage of digital reinvention is about actively seeking out ways to change and innovate. These companies are the early adopters in an industry or region. A proactive organization realizes that it is digital-first and is continually looking to the future. It often has a dedicated team of digital disruptors in the organization who are tasked with staying up-to-date on relevant emerging technologies. The process is lean and it enables staff through training and accountability. Its marketing team is the first to experiment with new ad platforms or social networks. The sales team implements and tests new additions to their sales tech stack. Most of these changes are driven by a desire to be customer centric.

The proactive stage looks at technology and asks how it could create a new process or path to the marketplace. It's not just about enhancing existing processes and systems. Technology adoption is a constant in this organization. Any new technology that is implemented comes with a new set of KPIs for the team that is using it. The proactive reinvention stage is about seeing trends early and having the culture and systems to embrace them quickly and efficiently.

STAGE 5 - REINVENTION LEADER

This is an aspirational stage and only a small portion of organizations fall into this category. Organizational structures tend to be flatter in these organizations. They could be the first in their industry to build a new technology platform connecting vendors with consumers. Think Amazon or eBay: they look at technologies outside of their industry or region and invest in ways that they can laterally implement it. They were the first to implement remote workforces, for instance, not out of necessity but out of curiosity, "What would happen if we built a virtual company with no physical offices?" "What if?" is a big part of their culture; a leadership-driven culture that drives and celebrates experimentation in tech, marketing, operations, and distribution.

A reinvention leader looks at emerging technology and combines it with another to drive a new business result or structure. It has people and processes in place that implement or create new tech, experiment, iterate, and then have the ability and power to scale it. Reinvention doesn't just happen in technology; it can be reinventing a sales process, a food product, or an organizational culture. This stage requires evolved leaders and organizational structures that promote innovation and risk taking as well as celebrate inclusion and diversity.

CHOOSING YOUR PATH OF REINVENTION

You must consciously and proactively choose your path of reinvention. It starts with having an honest understanding of where you are currently. If you're in stages 1-3, your business isn't future-proof. In fact, many of the organizations that did not weather the pandemic well were in those stages. It doesn't mean that being in stage 4 or 5 guarantees success, but you will at least have a fighting chance. Here are some real-world success stories:

QED Hospitality, a New Orleans-based company with 8 restaurants was like tens of thousands of other restaurants prohibited from allowing dine-in service during the peak of the pandemic. It ramped up its pick-up and take-out service using food delivery apps, as did its competition, but its story doesn't end there. The company had invested heavily in staff training, particularly in the area of customer service.

The award-winning customer-centric culture led to a highly engaged team, with low staff turnover.

The owners of QED were worried about the financial and emotional well-being of their 175 waiters and bartenders. Ideally, they wanted to retain them when dining services are eventually allowed to resume. The owners learned that about a new initiative to convert in-person doctor visits to telehealth (video-based calls) to lessen the burden on hospitals. The initial requirement was to quickly staff up 250 people in a virtual call center. The restaurateurs immediately created a new company called QED Resources as a staffing agency to provide telehealth customer service agents for the virtual call center. QED Resources hired 107 of their furloughed restaurant staff and after 5 days of video conference training to learn the related technology, they started working full-time from their homes and being paid as much as or more than their old wage. The entire team now engages in daily video conferences for a quick check-in, energy boost, and micro-training sessions similar to the pre-shift meetings they used to do before a busy night at the restaurants. The QED staff consistently score very highly on performance metrics set by the virtual call center. Just as bartenders hear tales over the rail and waiters chat up dinner parties, QED staff are now listening to stories from patients stuck at home while they guide them through the technical details of video calls and hospital patient portals.

Not only did the owners reinvent themselves, tap into tech, and create a new revenue-generating business, they helped their teammates find employment and maintained daily connection with them. When the staff were recently asked about the potential of returning to the restaurant, 95% want to return and 100% were grateful to their employer for caring about them. This means they will need to hire more people to keep both enterprises running. The staffing agency is positioned to scale for massive growth, as more hospitals and medical care organizations move to tele-health. This a good example of both Proactive Digital Reinvention and Reinvention Leadership.

Another pandemic example is the fate of the cruise ship industry in comparison to **Airbnb**. The cruise ship industry hasn't meaningfully changed in decades —it operates in an asset-heavy, unleveraged business model. On the other hand, Airbnb owned very few properties and leveraged technology and tens of thousands of independent homeowners. When the crisis struck, Airbnb was able to modify its model, reduce fixed costs, and serve a legitimate need in the marketplace. The biggest reason for this was its flexible, platform-based business model and culture of innovation. The cruise ship business is not as agile.

Walmart is in 27 countries and was already heavily invested in ecommerce and digital initiatives in 10 of those markets. It couldn't be called a true digital-first organization, but much of its marketing, recruitment, systems, and of course, ecommerce divisions are digital-first. When the pandemic crisis struck, it relied heavily on its ecommerce presence, even ramping up the number of items sold by partnering with Shopify, opening up the platform to thousands of Shopify vendors. One store alone in Renfrew, Ontario quickly ramped up to a full-time staff of 20 people dedicated to fulfilling ecommerce orders and e-customer engagement.

Walmart's resilience in turbulent times is rooted in its proactive investment in reinvention. Its incubator arm, "Store No8," is mandated to help Walmart focus on the future of retail by creating new operational efficiencies, leveraging technology, and unlocking amazing customer experiences. This brings elements of stage 4 and 5 digital reinvention into play. Notable retailers that are stage 2 or 3 who are in bankruptcy or closing locations en masse include David's Tea, GNC, Starbucks, The GAP, Victoria's Secret, BOSE, and hundreds of other major retailers.

Sprott Shaw College, located in Vancouver, British Columbia Canada, is the province's oldest career college, founded in 1903 with 16 campuses across the province. It adapted quickly to the crisis by transition to online learning rather than closing its doors to the public. With minimal staff adjustments, the college rolled out a rapid digital transformation plan that retained enrollment numbers while moving online.

The Admission Advisors who enroll students in-person were transitioned to work from their remote offices or homes using WebEx. The company invested in training to get their teams up-to-speed on how to support, enroll, and educate students virtually. All faculty moved to online live-class instruction. The enrollment process was also moved to the web. It was a big task, but they got it done. Most importantly, students were able to acquire important designations and further their careers. Not only did they survive the crisis, they broke enrollment records that had been in place for decades.

The Canadian Professional Sales Association has been in business for over 150 years and was originally started as a sales professional's travel discount association. 150 years later they have 20,000 members across Canada and their ranks include most major fortune 500's and leading sales organizations in every part of the country.

In 2018, the CPSA looked at how they were delivering their training and initiated an online learning focused mandate. They wanted to accelerate their investment in partners that deliver online sales training as well as wanted the CPSA to develop their own online sales training programs for their Certified Sales Professional designations. With that said, when the pandemic hit in March of 2020, the preceding sixty days had very low enrollments for training.

Because they had already invested in their online capabilities and were truly in the proactive reinvention phase, they were able to quickly reallocate many of their resources to the marketing and delivery of their online programs. They also leveraged that content through their educational partners across the country. Sure enough, by June 2020 they had one of their top months for enrollments. Without being able to offer travel discounts (because no salespeople were traveling), they were still able to add enough value to retain their members as they renewed their annual membership. The CPSA is also well positioned to weather future storms economically and be nimble as an organization. Their organization and team members are now well versed in the art and science of working and selling remotely, while still servicing their 20,000-member base across Canada.

When we reached out to the CPSA to learn more about their digital-first strategy, Nicolas Crowe, Vice President, Learning Solutions had this to share with us:

"Working remotely under these circumstances means adapting to a new environment and at the CPSA, we've prioritized communication and collaboration using Microsoft Teams. From virtual project management to team building events, we've completely shifted our mindsets to include effective virtual communication and collaboration in our new culture while stabilizing and maintaining productivity.

We identified a need to strengthen digital and technological fluency in the sales community with the lack of face-to-face meetings during the pandemic. It can be difficult to shift focus on how to build effective virtual presentations and communicate online, but in the early stages of the pandemic we provided free, weekly webinars to help sales professionals learn about the key concepts and skills they need adapt to the new environment of selling."

The VP of Sales of the very near future is one-part people developer and one-part CTO. They need to lead people and lead technology adoption and change.

> The VP of Sales of the very near future is one-part people developer and one-part CTO. They need to lead people and lead technology adoption and change.

THE DIGITAL-FIRST ENTERPRISE METRICS MODEL™

They say, "You can't improve what you can't measure." Any successful organization has systems to gauge its performance. The problem is that most of them are using traditional measuring standards in today's digital economy.

The word "metric" refers to a system or standard of measurement. A metric for businesses is a data-based measure used to gauge how well a specific business process is doing relative to its pre-set target. In 2011, Denis created his METRICS Model™ as a holistic way to set organizational wide key performance indicators (KPIs). As we enter the digital economy, we have updated his model to identify the seven key areas that need to be measured across the entire digital-first enterprise to gauge how well it is doing and where improvements need to be made. All of these metrics must arise from the organization's strategic objectives. These strategic objectives must be aligned with the company's core values, and the core values need to reflect the mission and vision of the enterprise.

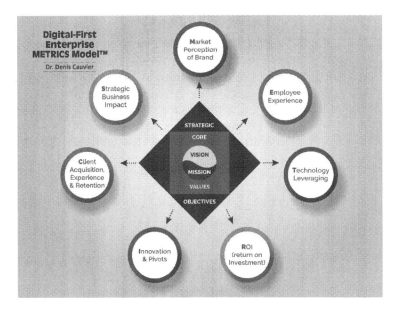

The example below illustrates how each of the seven key areas can be broken down to a handful of strategic KPIs:

M = Market Perception of Brand

- Thought Leadership, top-of-mind recall, and sentiment of brand. (Frequency of messages, overall "share of voice" in your space, perception of quality, value of products/services, and client care, perceptions of brand by community, impact on environment, employer of choice, and commitment to diversity)

E = Employee Experience

- Recruitment, selection, engagement, development, training, retention, and exit experience

T = Technology Leveraging

- Digital maturity (*Social IQ and EQ*)
- Adoption of tools for remote work
- Leveraging the best digital platforms and tools
- Ecommerce

R = ROI (Return on Investment)

- Return on ad spend
- Average revenue per account
- ROI on virtual training initiatives
- ROI on software

I = Innovation and Pivots

- Seeking and acquiring technology and trends insights
- Number of successful innovative ideas being implemented
- Number of successful products/ services launched
- Number of successful business models adopted for different markets
- Number of successful applications, technologies, and innovative solutions created
- Number of successful methodologies or adaptation launched

C = Client Acquisition, Experience, and Retention

- Traffic
- Cost per lead
- Lead conversion rates
- New customer acquisition rate and costs
- User experience
- Customer participation in digital channels
- Net Promoter Score (likelihood of a client refering/promoting your brand.)
- Customer lifetime value
- Social and digital performance

S = Strategic Business Impact
- ROI on marketing in digital channels
- Market share in targeted markets
- Percentage of revenue growth via digital channels
- Cross-departmental support for digital initiatives

This is not a comprehensive set of KPIs. It will vary based upon your core mission, vision, values, and strategic objectives. The METRICS model works once you have taken the time to decide which KPIs are most relevant to your situation.

Throughout the rest of this book, we'll be diving into the specifics on how you can improve your METRICS KPI's. Real results that can be achieved by adopting a digital-first enterprise model include;

- Strong brand awareness, perception and loyalty
- Respect as a responsible corporate citizen and member of the community
- Seen as an employer of choice with a commitment to diversity
- Sustainable business practices and reducing carbon footprint
- Recruit, develop and retain top talent
- Develop highly productive & engaged workforce
- Obtain high ROI on tech investments
- Pivot to new systems, methods, products, services or markets that drive the bottom line
- Increase market share, total revenues, client experience & client referrals/promoting
- Growth of online visibility and customer communities
- Reduce cost to attract and retain clients
- Increase net profits and share valuations.

Now that we have defined what digital-first is and you have a general idea of what stage your organization is in the digital transformation and you know what KPIs need to be measured, let's dive into the details of how to get real results.

CHAPTER 2

THE VIRTUAL LEADER

The move towards the work from home model is the natural evolution of the 4th Industrial Revolution. The global pandemic only sped up the inevitable. Recent statistics on remote work paint an interesting picture, you will find that in countries like the U.S., there was a 43% increase in people working remotely from 2015 to 2019. Even with the global sudden switch to virtual team's research that 38% of U.S. companies enjoyed gains in observed productivity and that 84% of businesses will likely increase their work-from-home capacity beyond the pandemic.

Some industries such as Computer, IT, Finance, Medical, Health, Sales, and Education were earlier adopters of the work-from-home model while others are still struggling. In the short-term you will see many hybrid models such as, some organizations' workforce returning to work, some working from home, and while others split time between the two. If a major second wave of the pandemic hits or if no cure/vaccine is created in the near future, this will continue to accelerate the work from home model to the new normal. Further advances in robotics, AI, Big Data, and Machine Learning will shorten the adoption curve.

The role of the leader for guiding a digital-first team in a virtual economy has become critical to a company's success given the recent massive global move to remote work. Although the fundamental principles of leading human beings have not changed, it is vital to learn how to do so in a virtual environment. As physical location no longer limits companies, they are in the unique position to hire the best talent regardless of their location while improving efficiency by working across time zones. A recent survey conducted by the Institute for Corporate Productivity compared the amount of remote work that was happening in various American based SME's just before COVID-19 outbreak and the results just several months later.

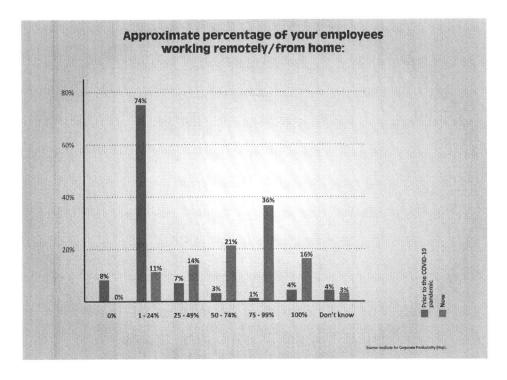

Many companies still resist the remote working model. They could be stuck in the previous century where organizations invested heavily on how to work effectively and efficiently in an office or because the nature of their work doesn't allow them to work from remote locations. Your core team may not be remote but your partners, clients, and value-added suppliers or contractors. Whether we like it or not, we are going to have to engage and lead people remotely. We would like to challenge you to start considering the various benefits to your company if you adopted a virtual team model.

Given the explosion of remote teams around the world we need to ensure that virtual leaders are up to the task. The following is a quick assessment tool that virtual leaders and aspiring virtual leaders can conduct on themselves. It can be used by team members to assess their leader as a form of 360 feedback. This could be feedback from your team, other leaders in the organization, clients or suppliers, and partners.

VIRTUAL LEADER SELF-ASSESSMENT

For each statement, rate your organization on a scale of 1-5 where:
1 = Strongly disagree 2 = Disagree 3 = Neutral 4 = Agree 5 = Strongly agree

Statement	1	2	3	4	5
We use defined digital-first KPIs.					
Our organization has a digital-first mindset.					
We manage our virtual teams differently than our traditional teams.					
We have trainings on best practices in effective virtual team leadership.					
We possess the digital fluency to lead, communicate, and collaborate with virtual teams.					
We have strong relationships, cooperation, trust, and team spirit within our virtual team.					
We are good at attracting, recruiting, and selecting top virtual team talent.					
We are good at onboarding, training, developing, and mentoring remote team members.					
We are good at engaging and motivating top virtual team talent.					
We are good at managing and providing performance feedback on work tasks, projects, and processes.					
We have the right tech tools to effectively lead virtual teams.					
Our leadership employs best practices and leads by example in the use of digital tools, platforms, and communications software.					
We have a clear understanding of the required core digital competencies of each team member.					
We have clear goals, direction, and priorities.					
We have clear roles among team members.					

Although managing remote teams has been a standard practice for some organizations, for many, this is a completely new environment. It has many challenges associated with it. For example, how do you maintain productivity, engagement, training, people development, and performance feedback as well as the morale and corporate culture with employees that are brand new and sometimes struggling with this new form of working? The act of adopting a virtual strategy does not mean that strategy is always going to be executed well.

> *"There are both right and wrong ways to implement remote work. If you're holding back because you're only looking at the wrong examples, you are going to miss out on many rewards."*
>
> - LAUREL FARRER, FOUNDER OF THE REMOTE WORK ASSOCIATION.

Research from multiple studies shows on average highly productive and profitable digital-first organizations invest 4.5 times the amount on training and developing their management team on virtual leadership core competencies.

If you want to have the best results as a virtual leader you should seriously consider adopting the following best practices:

- Investing the time and the expense once it is safe to do so to gather virtual teams together for an in-person learning or team-building event, ideally once every quarter.
- Having virtual meetings that build and reinforce the team culture through check-ins, activators, brainstorming exercises, etc.
- Supporting and modeling the effective use of various virtual communication tools while providing needed training and support.
- Having a well-thought-out and properly executed virtual onboarding program to not only orient the new employee to the organization but to fully welcome them to their virtual team.
- Reviewing job descriptions and core competencies to make sure that they are properly aligned with the realities and requirements of the virtual team.
- Recruiting and selecting top talent that possesses the right mindset, skills, knowledge, core competencies, and experiences.
- Defining clear employment and working agreements that are suitable for today's remote worker. This includes social media and external communications guidelines.
- Setting rewards, bonuses, and incentives for virtual leaders that reflect effective virtual team outcomes.
- Holding leaders and their teams accountable for the Digital-first Enterprise METRICS that they contribute towards.

"Technology itself is not the silver bullet. Technology is an enabler. I think an important element that people don't talk about, is this notion of workers wanting to feel informed. Organizations must give people the confidence, transparency and information needed to be empowered. Tools alone don't solve that."

- MARK MADER, PRESIDENT AND CEO OF SMARTSHEET.

Typical Challenges of Virtual Team Leaders

- Ability to meet with virtual team members frequently
- Ability to monitor productivity, output, and results remotely
- Building rapport & long-term relationships with teammates
- Running effective virtual team meetings
- Keeping team members engaged and team morale high
- Coaching team members from a distance
- Holding team members accountable for results
- Getting poor performance back on track

Typical Challenges of Virtual Team Members

- Unplugging after work
- Loneliness
- Collaborating/communication
- Home distractions
- Different time zones
- Staying motivated
- Taking vacation time
- Poor WIFI or other tech issues

Highly successful virtual teams have taken the time to devise strategies to resolve these challenges listed above. Remote work statistics from Gallup in early 2020 show how employees feel about remote working:

- 78% of leaders think that flexible schedules and telecommuting are the best non-monetary employee retention strategy.
- 82% of U.S. businesses use flexible work conditions to promote work-life balance.
- 83% of workers when comparing similar job opportunities would select the one offering remote work over those that don't.
- 32% of job seekers feel remote working is more important than being given a more prestigious job title.
- 54% of workers would leave their job for one with more flexibility.
- 67% of employees say that a loss of flexibility would make them start thinking about looking for another job.
- Research finds that "optimal engagement … occurs when employees spend 60 to 80% of their time working off-site."
- 90% of employees say that flexibility in their work arrangements contributes positively to their morale.

Dr. Peter Hirst of MIT found that with an effective virtual leader, there are many benefits of remote teams.

- 90% reported their family and personal life improved.
- 85% said that their stress was reduced.
- 80% said that their morale and engagement improved.
- 62% felt more trusted and respected.
- 93% believed that collaboration was better than before.

Dr. Peter Hirst of MIT found that with an effective virtual leader, there are many benefits of remote teams.

- **90% reported their family and personal life improved.**
- **85% said that their stress was reduced.**
- **80% said that their morale and engagement improved.**
- **62% felt more trusted and respected.**
- **93% believed that collaboration was better than before.**

Remote Work Drives the Bottom Line
Recent remote work statistics by Gallup sums up that, "Job flexibility engages remote workers — which drives performance."

- Remote workers can be 25% more productive than their onsite colleagues.
- 86% of employees say they're most productive when they work alone, devoid of distractions like inefficient meetings, office gossip, or loud office spaces.
- 80% of respondents would be more loyal to their employers if they had flexible work options.
- Each remote worker would reduce real estate costs by $10,000/year on average.
- Employee turnover reduces by 26% for companies that allow remote work over those that don't offer that option.
- 24% of employees work remotely at least one day a month "to be happy and productive."
- 77% say that working remotely reduces their company operating costs.

VIRTUAL SOLUTIONS CREATE ENVIRONMENTAL IMPACT

With the planet facing multiple serious environmental challenges, businesses need to step up and be part of the solution. A great way that businesses can reduce their carbon footprint is by embracing remote work. By tapping into digital communications, most meetings with potential clients and team member can happen without any driving or flying involved. Think of the impact of tens of millions of people not burning fossil fuels daily!

> A recent Harvard Business Review study found that, "… that the most successful virtual leaders make it a habit to have frequent virtual water cooler chats about family, hobbies, and challenges with each of their teammates and maintain a digital open-door policy."

A recent Harvard Business Review study found that, "… that the most successful virtual leaders make it a habit to have frequent virtual water cooler chats about family, hobbies, and challenges with each of their teammates and maintain a digital open-door policy."

REMOTE WORKING TOOLS ASSESSMENT

For each statement, rate your organization on a scale of 1-5 where:
1 = Strongly disagree 2 = Disagree 3 = Neutral 4 = Agree 5 = Strongly agree

Remote Working Tools	1	2	3	4	5	Improvement Ideas
Landline Telephone						
Mobile Telephone						
Text						
Facetime						
WhatsApp, FB Messenger						
Chat						
VoIP						
Email						
Online Meetings (Zoom, WebEx, GoToMeeting, MS Teams, Skype, etc.)						
Social Collaboration (Sales Force, Yammer, Slack, Chanty, HubSpot)						
File Sharing (Dropbox, WeTransfer, Google Docs)						
Social Media (LinkedIn, Facebook, Twitter, Instagram)						
Note taking (Evernote, Slite, Notion, Einstein Voice)						
Survey Tools (Survey Monkey, Google Forms, Typeform)						
Project Management Software (MS Project, Asana, Monday, Trello, Basecamp)						
Marketing Reporting Tools (Google Analytics, Cyfe)						

COMMUNICATION IS CRITICAL DURING A DIGITAL TRANSFORMATION

The key to any transformation effort has been clear communications and it is no different for a digital transformation. Digital changes require a transformation story, which helps employees (and all other affected stakeholders) understand where the organization is headed, why it is reinventing its model, and why the transformation is important. Organizations that effectively tell their digital transformation story are three times more likely to succeed! Secondly, senior leaders need to create a sense of urgency within their teams that need the transformation, a practice where good communication is central. Other research suggests that when communicating transformation stories, successful organizations tend to relay a clear and emotionally evocative story than others do. To accomplish this, one must first articulate the big-picture outcome: "What does success at the end of this transformation look like, what key milestones exist along the way, and what KPIs will we use to measure it to be sure that we have arrived?" Your transformation story has to be delivered to all stakeholders impacted and in the context that is relevant for them. Stakeholders include senior management, frontline team members, customer, shareholders, creditors, suppliers, key partners, and the community as a whole.

Key components of an effective digital transformation story:

- The logical rationale for the transformation
- The emotionally evocative story of the benefits to the stakeholder
- Key digital initiatives that will be implemented with timelines
- Defined goals for use of new digitalization related tools technologies and applications
- New evolving best practices for how employees will digitally work and collaborate alongside external partners and stakeholders
- Specifics on how digitization will change overall business strategies
- New approaches to tap into digital solutions to meet customer needs and engage customers
- Set a hard stop or deadline for full adoption

BURNING THE DIGITAL BRIDGE

One way to make your digital transformation deadline real is to "burn the digital bridge."

Several years ago, Shane Gibson was hired to keynote at a conference for Corning Cable Systems, which is now Corning Inc.'s fiber optics division. Unbeknownst to Shane, he was about to witness a rapid digital transformation at the conference. It's important to note that your digital transformation method should be aligned with your organization's culture as well.

> One way to make your digital transformation deadline real is to "burn the digital bridge."

Corning Inc. at that time was recruiting the majority of their sales professionals from the ranks of the military, often hiring new army veterans and training them to be sales professionals. This culture, as you can imagine, was a high energy, disciplined, with a traditional hierarchical structure that functioned very effectively. Shane was brought in to speak about how to leverage social media to drive new sales opportunities. Everyone on the sales team was armed with a BlackBerry and a Lenovo notebook. Right after Shane's talk, one of the senior sales leaders mentioned that most of the networks he talked about weren't truly accessible or easy to navigate using the BlackBerry as a mobile tool.

The head of sales then asked the team to put their Lenovo's on their tables with their Blackberries on top and informed them that all their data had already been transferred to brand new iPhones and Apple MacBook Pros. They were to turn over their devices immediately. In a less traditionally hierarchal organization, you would have had a mutiny. In this effective yet rank-and-file sales organization with great faith in their leadership, everyone turned over their prized devices and were handed brand new iPhones and MacBook Pros and then were put through a three-hour training session on how to use these tools immediately to ensure they put these new habits into action. They had no choice because management had burned the digital bridge. By the cocktail reception that evening, members of the sales team were posting content online.

At a CRM conference in Washington DC, Farmers Insurance shared one of their digital transformation stories. They were implementing a new CRM and transitioning away from a legacy client management system. Initially, they had quite a challenge getting their staff to utilize the CRM: a lot of the data was incomplete and they didn't seem to be logging in at all. What senior management and the technology implementation team discovered was that some the staff that had been there for years knew how to get into the legacy system through a backdoor using prompts and shortcuts. The tech team quickly closed that back door so that the only way to access that client database was through the new CRM. Within days, adoption of the new CRM went from 20-30% to over 90%.

To create digital change, we need fully commit to implementing that change in our organization. It's about positively reducing the friction to get people to adopt and adapt by making outdated workflows or options less accessible.

FLEXIBILITY AND AUTONOMY OF WORK ARRANGEMENTS

The need for flexible working conditions is growing. The changing context of work is creating new challenges and opportunities that can only be dealt with by implementing flexible working arrangements.

The most common forms of flexible working are:

- Part-time working
- Gig working
- Work from home
- Job sharing
- Variable hours
- Compressed hours
- Sabbaticals/career breaks
- Staggered start/end times
- Dual roles
- Flexible benefits (buying/selling holiday time)

Flexible working arrangements drive employee engagement and real results by creating choices, accommodating individual needs, enabling complexity, and enabling agility. Companies can reduce their carbon footprint and long-distance travel for employees by implementing various flexible work arrangements. Flexible work arrangements reduce the need for expensive office space and corporate parking costs, while saving employees the cost and time of commuting. This flexibility allows for greater work/life balance. Virtual teams composed of staff from remote locations can deliver increased client expectations by providing 24/7 global customer care. Flexible and autonomous work arrangements with mature, responsible people can increase employee engagement, loyalty, and retention.

"If you are comfortable with the amount of freedom you have given your employees then you haven't gone far enough."

- LARRY PAGE, FORMER GOOGLE CEO

Agile Talent Management in its truest form is about giving everyone autonomy (the power) and flexibility (the freedom to choose how, when, and where they work). Numerous studies have shown that workplace flexibility and autonomy are the two most important predictors of workplace satisfaction. Whether it is control of one's place and time of work, or of the work environment, autonomy, and flexibility help engage and retain the best and brightest staff. New employees at Facebook are allowed to choose the team they want to join, upon completion of their onboarding program. Facebook has done away with tracking employee absenteeism. At Zappos, a concept called "holacracy" has replaced hierarchical structure with a series of self-governed teams that share authority and increase the speed and innovation of decision-making. Netflix's policy to managing vacation time is "There is no policy on tracking vacation time."

Today's successful virtual organizations have made the bold shift from tracking staff hours and whereabouts to tracking staff results and wellness. It's about providing a technology platform that doesn't just track results but enables, empowers, and encourages employees to leverage needed technologies on-demand.

CHAPTER 3

POSITION YOUR COMPANY AS AN EMPLOYER OF CHOICE IN THE DIGITAL WORLD

"70% of the global workforce is composed of passive talent."

– FINANCES ONLINE

Today's consumers are digitally connected like never before and demand high quality products from brands they can trust. They care deeply if the materials used were ethically sourced, manufactured, distributed, sold, and how sustainably the end of use (life) of the product will be handled. Consumers demand that the brands that they purchase from not only protect the environment, but also are committed to equity in pay and diversity in their workforce. These same concerns are paralleled when it comes to how the public views employers. Positioning your company as an employer of choice in the digital world means so much more than just paying your people well. It is an all-encompassing effort that begins with providing your existing employees a positive virtual experience from their first impressions of your employer branding, throughout the hiring process, and during their experiences as a team member right to the point of exiting the company.

ALWAYS ON STAGE DIGITALLY

Transparency and authenticity as a brand is no longer optional; we are always on stage digitally as enterprises and employers. If you onboard your employees poorly or you renege on a compensation plan. That is going to end up on the Internet. It doesn't matter if you have non-disclosure clauses or privacy clauses with your staff it'll just end up being posted online anonymously. The challenge is today people trust anonymous posters on the Internet more than they trust traditional enterprises or institutions. It is not just your word against theirs for you are often guilty until proven innocent, and the damage is almost always irreparable at that point. We need to operate as organizations as if someone is always watching and that everything we do, even through private or encrypted messages, can be screen captured and shared broadly. As enterprises, we are always on stage.

The hiring process for digital-first enterprises looks different from what most companies are used to. Businesses must now account for the recent overnight shift to virtual, which includes updated and revised talent acquisition processes. Agile digital interviewing and assessment solutions deliver efficiencies and predictive insights for multiple HR processes, including candidate assessment and prioritization. This chapter will provide you with proven strategies you can implement now to help your business effectively recruit, pre-screen, interview, and hire new employees as a remote team.

Transparency and authenticity as a brand is no longer optional; we are always on stage digitally as enterprises and employers. If you onboard your employees poorly or you renege on a compensation plan. That is going to end up on the Internet. It doesn't matter if you have non-disclosure clauses or privacy clauses with your staff it'll just end up being posted online anonymously.

Every company has a reputation and your company's reputation impacts how people perceive and speak about your organization, products, and services. That reputation is known as your brand, your brand must have a strong awareness of the areas that you do business in. It's not about how you're viewed as an employer, by current and former employees but by potential employees and the public in general. Without addressing your multidimensional online brand and stakeholders, hiring and retaining the best employees to maintain your strategic market advantage becomes very challenging and costly. It doesn't matter how much money you spend, if you don't do this well you can't attract and retain top talent.

Sharing a strong employer brand is more than good storytelling, it's about authentically delivering the employee experience that is in line with how you want your organization to be perceived in the marketplace. Your best online marketing and branding comes from the stories that customers, employees, and former employees tell about your brand. Satisfied and engaged employees are your best recruiters, particularly in an age of social media. What's interesting is that simple and practical actions to improve your employees' experience will not only create positive sentiment about your company as an employer but it will have a quick impact on morale and performance of your current team. This will in turn attract motivated job seekers and an army of happy employees. Happy and engaged staff are constantly broadcasting their positive experience that re-enforces your employer brand to their networks which can include passive job seekers.

Employer Branding Statistics

- 96% of companies believe employer brand and reputation impacts revenue. (CareerArc)

- 78% of job candidates say the overall candidate experience they get is an indicator of how a company values its people. (Talent Adore)
- When deciding where to apply for a job, 84% of job seekers say the reputation of a company as an employer is important. (TalentNow)
- Employee turnover can be reduced by 28% by investing in the employer brand. (Office Vibe)
- 86% of U.S. women and 67% of U.S. men wouldn't join a company with a bad reputation. (CRO Magazine)
- Negative reviews of products and services are the #1 factor damaging employer brands. (CareerArc)
- 92% of people would consider changing jobs if offered a role with a company with an excellent corporate reputation. (CR Magazine)
- 49% of employers believe they don't have the tools to effectively enhance employer brand. (CareerArc)

EMPLOYEE "VIRTUAL EXPERIENCE" ARE YOU REFERABLE?

Imagine receiving poor service and undercooked food at a restaurant. As you pay for your meal, the manager says, "I hope you will encourage your friends and family to come check us out. If they do, we will give you a coupon for a free appetizer." Note that the manager makes this offer without enquiring about the quality of the food and service you received. This example is similar to the way many companies implement employee referral programs. They offer a token referral bonus to encourage their employees to recruit friends and family members into an organization that is less than stellar. It should come as no surprise that this approach to employee referrals has unspectacular results.

IT'S ALL ABOUT THE EXPERIENCE

If you want a stronger employer brand, you first need to make sure you are giving your employees something positive to share.

The following slogan shared to Denis by one of his mentors (and Shane's father) Bill Gibson, applies to both the world of customer service and to creating an organization that employees will be proud to share with others, "People will go to where they are *invited*, will stay when they are *appreciated*, and will *Invite* others when encouraged to do so!" To turn your workforce into a team of recruiters, you need to take an honest look at the work experience you deliver.

REGARDLESS OF THE EXPERIENCE, THEY WILL TALK

Understanding what the actual work experience you provide your employees with is a very valuable exercise. If the feedback is not stellar the priority would be to make immediate improvements which will lead to a more engaged and productive team. If the feedback is resoundingly positive, that's great in that not only are your teammates happy but they can be encouraged to share this with their networks on social media. By investing the time and energy to create work experiences that are engaging, inspiring, and collegial, your workforce becomes an army of recruiters, it also improves morale, productivity, engagement, and customer service quality.

The following tool is meant to provide you a quick analysis of how well your organization delivers in terms of ten key employee experiences.

SELF-CHECK – 10 KEY EMPLOYEE E.X.P.E.R.I.E.N.C.E.S ™

The following self-check will get you started with an analysis of the work experience your company delivers. Here is how to use it for maximum benefit:

1. Use the experiences as a starting point to generate a more complete checklist defining the total employee experience at your company.

2. Use the questions under each experience to analyze how you can improve the way you deliver that experience.

Entering the organization (Onboarding)	Yes	No
Is your orientation program inspiring?		
Does your onboarding program leave new hires with the impression that you're a well-run, professional company that does things right?		
Do new hires feel valued and that company cares about their well-being and success?		
Does your orientation program reinforce recruits' decision to join the company?		
Is our organization leveraging technology effectively to provide the best onboarding experience for recruits?		
X Exiting experience	Yes	No
Was the real reason for a person's leaving identified?		
Was every reasonable effort made for both parties to part on positive terms?		
Were opportunities for internal improvements noted, communicated, and implemented?		
Is our organization leveraging technology effectively to learn from the employee exit and maintain the person as a brand advocate?		
Performance management and feedback	Yes	No
Do employees receive regular performance feedback?		
Do supervisors and managers know how to give feedback in clear, concrete terms?		
Do supervisors and managers know how to give corrective feedback respectfully?		
Do supervisors and managers know how to invite employees to share their point of view, so they feel understood?		
Do supervisors and managers integrate these conversations into the employee's development plan?		
Are performance evaluations seen as a useful performance enhancement and professional development tool?		
Does the performance evaluation reflect previous performance and detail the plan for moving forward?		

Performance management and feedback	Yes	No
Are employees' active participants in the review process and assessing their own performance?		
Is our organization leveraging technology effectively to provide highly effective performance management feedback?		

Engagement levels	Yes	No
Overall, are the employees satisfied with their job?		
Overall, are the employees satisfied with their employer?		
Overall, are the employees satisfied with their boss?		
Overall, are the employees satisfied with their co-workers?		
Is our organization leveraging technology effectively to assess, build, and enhance employee engagement in real-time?		

Recruitment process	Yes	No
Do your recruitment efforts attract a large number of high-quality candidates?		
Do your recruitment efforts make applicants feel respected?		
Does your recruitment efforts reinforce a positive employer brand?		
Does the job offer clearly state the job being offered (start date and time, pay, and benefits)?		
Does the welcome package provide valuable information for the new recruit to review before the first day on the job?		
Is our organization leveraging technology effectively to recruit a diverse and highly talented pool of applicants?		

Individual development plan and mentoring	Yes	No
Does each employee have an individual development plan?		
Does the organization have a systemized coaching process?		
Are individualized training need assessments conducted on each employee before training begins?		
Is a learning culture part of the organization?		
Does the company measure its ROI on training and development efforts?		
Is our organization leveraging technology effectively to develop, mentor, coach all employees, and track the ROI on those efforts?		

Employee referrals and advocacy	Yes	No
Is there a structured employee referral program in place?		
Are employees aware of the employee referral program?		
Is the process for referring someone easy to do?		
Does the company quickly act upon the referral provided, by contacting the referred person?		
Does the employee who provided the referral get acknowledged in some way?		
Is there a formalized process to provide thanks after a referral is given and a reward after new employee passes probation?		
Is our organization leveraging technology effectively to run their employee referral and reward systems?		

Networking with colleagues	Yes	No
Are cross-departmental communications among colleagues encouraged?		
Has every effort been made to ensure "silos" don't develop within the organization? If they develop are they removed?		
Are colleagues from distant locations networking via video conferencing not just email and text?		
Does a culture of mutual respect exist with all colleagues regardless of position?		
Can all employees access senior leaders?		
Does your colleague networking showcase people with high potential?		
Is our organization leveraging technology effectively to facilitate professional networking and personal relationship development with colleagues?		
Communications with leader	**Yes**	**No**
Do employees feel comfortable to raise disagreements with their boss?		
Do employees feel that honesty and transparency is valued and encouraged?		
Do employee concerns get addressed?		
If an employee concern doesn't result in change, is an explanation provided?		
Are employee's ideas and input highly valued?		
Are employees advised of the status of their ideas? If an idea isn't used, do they understand why?		
Do managers know how to create an open and safe environment?		
Are managers held accountable for how they treat their employees?		
Are employees kept in the loop during change processes?		
Is our organization leveraging technology effectively to foster effective communications?		
Equity, Inclusion, and Diversity	**Yes**	**No**
Is there equity and diversity at all levels in the organization?		
Is the culture one in which employees are not expected to work after they leave work or is there a restriction on how many hours are expected of any employee in a given week?		
Is the focus on outcomes, not hours worked?		
Are healthy breaks (exercise, stretching, or standing) promoted throughout the workday?		
Is extra time off for charitable pursuits or volunteer work offered?		
Do you ask employees what work/ life balance means to them?		
Do you offer programs, education, coaching, and incentives for employee wellness and work life balance?		
Is our organization leveraging technology effectively to create equity, diversity, and employee wellness for all employees?		

3.   Ask the following questions for each "E.X.P.E.R.I.E.N.C.E.":

- o   What do our employees say they want from each **E.X.P.E.R.I.E.N.C.E.** interaction?
- o   How do our employees feel and see things after dealing with each **E.X.P.E.R.I.E.N.C.E.** interaction as they are told?
- o   How would our employees feel if we instructed them to deal with **E.X.P.E.R.I.E.N.C.E.** interactions differently?
- o   What emotions and perceptions should we be trying to create in our employees, and what do we need to do to create them?

4.   You can start by asking your employees:

- o   "Does your work experience to date want you to vocally appreciate it within social circles?"

5.   It's not enough just to involve employees in data gathering, but you also need their valuable input and assisting in implementing changes. As for any change or corporate initiative, the more you involve your employees in the process, the more invested they'll be in it. Higher levels of investment result in better data, and better data leads to more productive recruitment of talent.

Where does the responsibility for employer branding lie? Traditionally people thought it was the president of a small business, or in larger companies the HR, communications, or marketing departments that create the employer brand. The reality is, your brand is not what your website says it is. Like it or not, employer branding starts and ends ultimately with your employees and the experiences that they collectively create for their fellow teammates. As these experiences will drive comments on social media sites, job reviews, and testimonials, during conversations and in networking settings, all of which will impact your company's reputation.

RECRUITING IS BROADCASTING

Recruiting is an essential element of attracting quality employees. Recruiting is a form of marketing since it's a process of selling a job opportunity to prospective employees. Recruiters need to be honest about what the position entails and avoid overselling candidates on the company; overselling can lead to disillusionment and, eventually, to staff turnover. It can also result in recruits accusing the company of false advertising, a charge that can damage the firm's reputation and hamper future recruitment efforts. Recruitment activity should be creative, imaginative, honest, and innovative. Proper word choice in recruiting materials is essential. For instance, avoid describing your company as simply large or established; descriptors like rapidly expanding, nationally known, or leading, are more dynamic, and are more likely to appeal to quality candidates. Also, the style of recruiting material should be simple and direct, always shedding light on the candidate's primary question of, "What's in it for me?" In this vein, do not forget to personalize your material by using pronouns like "you" and "your." Finally, you should never lose sight of the fundamental objectives of your recruitment campaign.

Typically, there are five main objectives for recruitment messages:

1. To attract suitable candidates for the job
2. To eliminate inappropriate candidates
3. To motivate many appropriate candidates to apply
4. To reach the best people as economically as possible
5. To enhance the overall reputation and brand of the company by the image projected in the recruitment material

No single recruitment technique is effective at all times, under all circumstances, and for all companies. Most companies have found they must be prepared to adapt their methods to the constantly changing nature of the labor market.

TIMING IS EVERYTHING

Dr. John Sullivan says that the timing of the recruiting message is as important as the message itself when targeting top prospects. Passive job seekers are more receptive to recruiting messages under certain circumstances. In sales we would call these trigger events. He offers the following suggestions related to "right timing" under different circumstances:

- Birthdays and New Year's Day are times of reflection
- A boss, mentor, best friend, or CEO left the company
- Day of a merger or layoff announcement
- Lost a promotion or a key project
- After their yearly bonus
- After their performance appraisal
- When their project is ending
- Their annual work anniversary

DON'T INVITE THE WRONG PEOPLE

One of the worst things to do is to attract the wrong people to apply for your job postings. Not only will you be disappointed if you hire the wrong person, but you overload your pre-screening process with ill-fitting candidates. Virtual teams require people who are self-sufficient and excellent communicators so these are the types of people you need to attract with your recruiting efforts.

Effective leadership communication within virtual teams is often the biggest challenge. By default, virtual team communication is electronic, which means you can miss out on the nonverbal cues we rely on for effective exchanges. Removing face-to-face communications can negatively impact the quality of collaboration which erodes morale and diminishes results.

Don't be too quick to automatically rule out a candidate who hasn't worked on a virtual team, if they possess the characteristics and remaining core competencies you have identified, you might have a high potential individual. Realize that if you do hire them, they will likely require training and guidance to communicate effectively over a virtual medium.

Many forward-thinking employers are recruiting for skills and interests that traditionally may have been seen as a liability. These are in the areas of online gaming, game development, or personal time spent on social channels. They are finding that gamers who coordinate teams, or guilds in massive multiplayer games, are already immersed and competent in the virtual team environment.

Many have self-organized and custom-built communications platforms and servers just to enhance game play. Shane's son, Kristian Gibson, and his close network of friends have collaboratively pooled funds, developed gaming servers, and leveraged messaging platforms such as Discord to create what looks a lot like a best-of-breed virtual working community. The Discord server even leverages bots and AI to make them more efficient. These types of employees come ready to engage and collaborate with your team. Contrary to many parents' opinions, spending hours each day gaming can actually be a great investment in your future.

Julian Lee, CEO of ChannelNext and EChannelNews said it well when he said, "People don't know what being truly digital-first is about, the next wave of employees and entrepreneurs are seasoned digital veterans, Gen Z can play a video game for 11 hours straight without eating. They can document a 5-hour event live on social platforms, while having 3 text conversations, and engaging in real life at the event." If we are resistant to investing time on digital while our competitors are immersed in it, there's not much of an opportunity to develop our digital fluency.

ASSESSING DIGITAL READINESS FOR EMPLOYEES

The following model was created to help identify how a person ranks on the Digital-first INNER STRENGTHS Core Traits Assessment and provides insights on how well they will likely perform within a high functioning virtual team.

Whether you wish to assess the digital readiness of a potential candidate for hire or assessing a long-standing employee, it's critical to determine which individuals are resilient and can learn the needed competencies to perform well in the ever changing virtual economy. The best employees of the digital world have the following core traits and the acronym "INNER STRENGTHS" is an easy way to remember them:

DIGITAL-FIRST INNER STRENGTHS CORE TRAITS ASSESSMENT

Innovative
Networker
Nimble and agile
Enquiring mindset
Relationship builder

Stretch beyond comfort zones
Teachable mindset
Resilience during adversity

Emotional maturity
Neutralizing negatives
Goal and project focused
Tenacity, discipline and action
Happiness, gratitude and enthusiasm
Success driven

A powerful and practical way to adopt this tool for your organization is to fill out the following chart.

SAMPLE COMPETENCY BASED INTERVIEW QUESTIONS

Competency: Nimble and Agile	
Please describe a significant change you have had to deal with at work recently.	
Possible follow up questions:	• What was your initial reaction to the change? • How did it work out?
Notes:	

DIGITAL-FIRST INNER STRENGTHS CORE TRAITS ASSESSMENT

Candidate: _____ Interviewer: _____

Core Trait: Innovative	
Behavioral question:	
Possible follow up questions:	
Notes:	

Core Trait: Networker	
Behavioral question:	
Possible follow up questions:	
Notes:	

Core Trait: Nimble and agile
Behavioral question:

Possible follow up questions:	

Notes:

Core Trait: Enquiring mindset
Behavioral question:

Possible follow up questions:	

Notes:

Core Trait: Relationship builder
Behavioral question:

Possible follow up questions:	

Notes:

Core Trait: Stretch beyond comfort zones
Behavioral question:

Possible follow up questions:	

Notes:

Core Trait: Teachable mindset
Behavioral question:

Possible follow up questions:	
Notes:	

Core Trait: Resilience during adversity
Behavioral question:

Possible follow up questions:	
Notes:	

Core Trait: Emotional maturity
Behavioral question:

Possible follow up questions:	
Notes:	

Core Trait: Neutralizing negatives
Behavioral question:

Possible follow up questions:	
Notes:	

Core Trait: Goal and project focused
Behavioral question:

Possible follow up questions:	
Notes:	

Core Trait: Tenacity, discipline, and action
Behavioral question:

Possible follow up questions:	
Notes:	

Core Trait: Happiness, gratitude, and enthusiasm
Behavioral question:

Possible follow up questions:	
Notes:	

Core Trait: Success driven
Behavioral question:

Possible follow up questions:	
Notes:	

To get the best results from the **Digital-first INNER STRENGTHS Core Traits Assessment** first take the time to assess your current employees on each of the 14 core traits. Identify any areas for development and proceed with appropriate training and or mentoring. This may be a difficult but necessary reality check for you and your team. If you have team members who are scoring low in many vital areas and they lack the digital fluency or will to evolve, they may need to be supported and encouraged to seek opportunities that are more aligned with their skillsets.

The second way to use this tool is for the recruiting and selection of future teammates.

> "59 % of HR leaders say their organizations don't have a defined set of skills needed for their digital transformation."
>
> *- AON'S 2020 DIGITAL READINESS REPORT*

> *"Tolerance, intercultural dialogue and respect for diversity are more essential than ever in a world where people are becoming more and more closely interconnected."*
>
> *- KOFI ANNAN*

Recruiting Top Virtual Team Talent Faster

ESTABLISH RECRUITING KPIS

Below are some recruiting, pre-screening, and selection KPIs worth considering. Select 6 to 8 of the most important for your company to track and evaluate to ensure your recruiting process is as effective as it can be.

- Increase in active seekers
- Talent pipeline growth
- Percentage of applications from referrals
- Increase of quality applications received
- *Glassdoor, Indeed, Great Place to Work,* and other employer review ratings
- Balance of recruiter-led content vs. content from employees and peers
- Percentage of first choice candidates accepted rate
- Percentage of new hires retained beyond formal onboarding period
- Application drop off rate
- Candidate satisfaction rate
- Employee turnover rate
- Percentage of employees participating in employee referral program
- Time to fill
- Time to accept
- Time to start
- Time to finish initial orientation
- Number of qualified applicants per opening
- Percentage submitted vs. accepted by hiring manager
- Submitted short list candidates to hire rate

- Hiring manager satisfaction rate
- Source of hire
- ROI for source of hire (or digital channel)
- New hire failure rate
- Cultural fit – 360 assessment
- Source of applicant ROI
- Source of hire ROI
- ROI on TA initiatives
- HR department budget per full time employee
- Cost to "productivity/proficiency"
- Percentage of new hires that become innovators or top performers
- Improvement in the performance of new hires over existing/former jobholders
- Percentage of projects delayed/missed due to lack of talent
- High performance employee retention for key and hard to fill positions
- Number of successors developed for strategic positions
- Performance of new hires vs. older employees in same role
- Percentage of goals attained

YOU CAN'T HIT A TARGET YOU CAN'T SEE

Imagine trying to shoot a bow and arrow at a target after a blind has been put over your eyes and you have been spun around multiple times? The likelihood of hitting the target with your arrow would be slim to none; you can't hit a target you can't see. The same holds true for recruiting great people. If you can't identify in advance what constitutes a perfect candidate, you are not likely to either attract them with your recruiting efforts nor recognize them as applicants. Job descriptions are useful tools that help us focus on our target: what key skills, knowledge, attitudes, and core competencies the successful candidate must have for us to consider hiring them. When people don't take the time to identify their target (by not having a quality job description prepared for the position), they often fall into a trap. Upon meeting an applicant that meets their basic criteria, they close their ears and turn their mouth on "auto sell." They close their mind to the screening process and focus all their energy on selling the position to this "wonderful" applicant, rather than examining how well this person will work within the virtual team.

CONSIDER EXISTING STAFF FIRST

One of the best ways to maintain a high level of staff morale and ensure employee loyalty is to promote internally. The benefits are multiple, firstly you already know how well they work within your corporate culture. You know their strengths and weaknesses. They already have developed professional relationships with teammates, clients, and suppliers. Once the word gets out that your company truly invests in its people by training and developing them through succession of jobs you will find that quality candidates will seek you out.

By demonstrating loyalty to your employees by promoting from within your teammates will reciprocate this loyalty back to the company. This approach makes employees feel that their capabilities, skills, and accomplishments are acknowledged and appreciated. They feel motivated to perform their duties diligently and responsibly. This means that we need to have a process and program in place to upskill and develop employees for future opportunities and positions before we need them.

EMPLOYEE REFERRAL PROGRAM

"Over 93% of the top performers in their field find a job by being referred by someone they know." - Forbes

GIVE ME 5

Google uses a very direct approach to employee referrals called "Give me 5." Under this policy, the company approaches top performers and asks them to identify the top five people that they know in their field in terms of performance, innovation, team orientation, management skill, and performance under pressure. the following categories:

- The best virtual team performer
- The most innovative virtual team member
- The best virtual team player
- The best virtual team leader
- The best virtual team member that works well under pressure

They then ask their top performers to reach out to these five individuals to try to convince them to apply for work at Google.

Employee referral programs enable you to leverage the employee's professional network to find the quality future teammates. Allowing your employees to refer someone they know works somewhat like a guarantee because they are being referred by someone you already trust. When your employees share the job opportunity, they normally provide a realistic insight as to what the position entails and the corporate culture.

Get your current employees to help get the word out by leveraging their social media and encourage them to share the job posting thus increasing the reach. Ideally, if staff are comfortable sharing why they love working for their company within the job opening post it will personalize the message.

Some of the types of content that are easy for employees to share include:

- Employee personal stories
- Community initiatives
- CEO content on leadership, company direction
- Profiling of suppliers
- Press coverage
- Employee content and thought leadership
- Innovative or unique product or service stories

Part of the role of a social recruitment team is to curate and aggregate content and make it easily shareable for staff. Many organizations will use a tool like LinkedIn Elevate, Oktopost, Bambu, Post Beyond, and Hootsuite Amplify to organize all sharable content in one place for employees to access. They track who's sharing and engaging with the company content. Some of these have different pricing, elements, and integration. If you're on a small budget, you can opt to write a weekly email digest of the top content you would like employees to share. It's advisable that sharing is a "suggestion" and not mandatory, for the term mandatory often deters employees from promoting the brand.

THERE'S NO PLACE LIKE HOME(PAGE)

There is little you can control on the Internet; however, you have complete control of your homepage. Make sure that your company's homepage is visually appealing, functional, user friendly, and ranks highly on all major search engines. It is imperative that your clients and potential customers can easily find you. This same thinking applies for potential future teammates. Since brand reinforcement starts at your website there is no place like home(page) to incorporate your new recruiting efforts. Every marketing expert will tell you that branding should be consistent throughout every possible touchpoint. What this means in this context is your "Careers" page needs to "look and feel" consistent with your home page, that is to say use your company logo, fonts, and standardized color schemes throughout.

One important thing to note is every page on your site is a homepage. When people use Google and search for a specific term, Google may send them to a specific page on your site, even a blog post could be the starting point for a visitor. If online recruitment is to be a priority, then every relevant page must have an easy to find link or call to action that sends them to your main recruitment section.

Online visitors should always be able to see a "Careers" link easily on any page without having to search for it. Research indicates that if the visitor must make more than three clicks to find what they want, they will likely move on and go elsewhere. Having a simple "Careers" or "Employment" tab or button directly on your main navigation, which links to a more detailed and seeker-focused Career Opportunities page will do. Once on the Careers page, visitors should be able to quickly locate clear information on current job openings and instructions on how to inquire. If the firm has few available openings, consider a generic "We're always interested in talking to future teammates" type of message, to encourage potentially passive seekers to either post the resume for the future or keep your company on their radar for future job searching. A one line, "We are not hiring" message can make your entire organization appear cold or unapproachable.

You may even want to think about having a careers newsletter or alerts via email or text. When a visitor arrives at a career page and stays for a specific time it can trigger a pop-up which encourages them to add their email, mobile number, or WhatsApp number to your careers email list for on-going updates. This can help develop a pool of people who understand your organization, its vision and culture. It can help drive referrals for relevant candidates if the content is made or updates are made easy to share.

Build and Maintain a Reserve Tank

If you are like most companies that have a pool of candidates who have previously submitted applications, you should take the time to revisit them as some may be still job hunting. There was something about your company that attracted them to previously apply. Why not maintain a relationship with previous applicants that you deem to be strong potential future candidates so you can create a solid reserve tank of talent for when you next need to hire? Beyond email and text subscriptions you can direct them to follow your organization on LinkedIn, Instagram, Facebook, and any other relevant platforms. If you're doing the interviewing, it's advisable to connect with any viable candidate you have met with via LinkedIn regardless of the outcome – keeping up to date with their activities may identify a change in their situation or build the trust needed to generate referrals from them.

MAKE THE PROCESS USER-FRIENDLY

The application experience will be for many candidate's, their first significant interaction with your company and this first impression goes a long way in re-enforcing the employer's brand or negating it. Applicants don't want to be part of a long and exhausting application process. Try to streamline the process, consider shortening your online forms, enable applicants to apply using their mobiles, and use QR Codes for instant connection to the application portal. Make sure that you immediately acknowledge the submission of an application. Use a chatbot to answer the most common questions. Inform applicants of the next steps and the time frame of when they are likely to hear back.

- Candidates don't want to complete an application that will take longer than 20 minutes. (*CareerBuilder*)
- 76% of job seekers want to know how long it's going to take to fill out an application before they start. (*CareerBuilder*)
- 66% of job seekers said they would wait only two weeks for a callback after which they consider the job a lost cause and move on to other opportunities. (*CareerBuilder*)

LEVEL THE PLAYING FIELD WITH SOCIAL MEDIA RECRUITING

Very few companies can out-spend the giants in their industry, however they can tap into social media and level the playing field when it comes to recruiting top talent. It's about out-engaging the big guys with the handful of ideal candidates that you want to bring onboard. As we said before, your company's brand and online reputation are **key** decision factors for all aspects of business growth including attracting, selecting, and retaining talent. With social media being a key factor in building and reinforcing your employer of choice branding. Social media recruiting is the practice of identifying, attracting, engaging, and hiring both active and passive candidates, by engaging them on the social networks they're already on. Denis has been a huge advocate of social media recruiting, his book *Hired 2.0 – Recruiting Exceptional Talent @ the Speed of Light* was released in early 2010 was the world's first book dedicated solely to this topic. By reviewing a candidate's social media profiles recruiters can get quick insights on the individual, their interests, and what they're seeking. Social media recruiting differs from other types of recruiting because it allows the recruiter to connect directly with both active and passive job seekers and have real-time online interactions.

The difference between searching for people on Google versus a social platform is significant. When you search a topic on Google you essentially find static web pages that the search engine algorithm feels are relevant. When you search a topic on Twitter, Instagram, or LinkedIn you get real human sentiment on a topic; it's what people are feeling and individually communicating right now, and you can engage those people in real-time in many cases.

Here are some employer branding stats as it relates to social media

- Social enterprises are 58% more likely to attract top talent and 20% more likely to retain them. (LinkedIn)
- 79% of job applicants use social media in their job search. (Glassdoor)
- 70% of hiring managers say they've successfully hired with social media. (Betterteam)
- 73% of millennials found their last position through a social media site. (Aberdeen Group)
- 71% of recruiters said social media recruiting was effective in decreasing time-to-fill for non-management, salaried positions. (SHRM)
- Job seekers rank social media and professional networks as the most useful job search resource compared to job boards, job ads, recruiting agencies, and recruiting events. (CareerArc)
- 75% of U.S. respondents believe that companies whose C-Suite executives and leadership team use social media to communicate about their core mission, brand values, and purpose are more trustworthy. (Glassdoor)
- Increasing employer brand and recognition comes second on the list of reasons why organizations use social media for recruitment, with 77% of survey respondents answering this way (preceded only by recruiting passive candidates with 82%). (SHRM)
- Employee voice is 3x more credible than the CEO's when it comes to talking about working conditions in that company. (Edelman Trust Barometer)

It's important to stay current and up to date with your job postings on your company's website and use social media to raise awareness of your career openings. By refreshing your job posts online, they will get more attention and more attention can drive more passive job seekers to apply online. You can find key candidates by engaging with them through shared passions, ideals or networks, something you can't do with the other recruitment methods.

Social media recruiting when done well has many advantages including:

- They are free or inexpensive to use
- The size of their user base means that you can connect with many people
- People spend a lot of time on them so there can be frequent exposure to your brand
- Most believe what they read on them (Credible)

47

- Less spam, so people use them in lieu of email
- They allow you to meet people that cannot be found on resume posting sites
- They are easy to learn and use
- They provide a global recruiting capability
- They can be used for pre-screening
- Can be used in conjunction with blogs, podcasts, and the corporate website
- Social networks are now accessible from smartphones (Continuous access)
- You can use them to counter negative images
- Most individuals list their job title and where they work in their profiles
- Most people provide valuable insights into their non-work interests
- They can add value during "slow" recruiting times
- Some allow you to easily add contacts by automatically searching your address book
- They can be fun

BEST PRACTICES OF SOCIAL MEDIA RECRUITING

One Site Does Not Fit All

If marketers want to communicate with a large audience, they will normally do so over multiple social media platforms. They understand that to obtain the right mix of frequency of message and type of message they need to engage their market using multiple digital tools. The same is true for social media recruiting, different sites have appeal to different markets and often appeal to the same market in different ways. It's interesting to note that what might work for Twitter won't necessarily translate to LinkedIn or Facebook.

Beware of cross posting the same updates generically. If you post the same video, at the same time to Instagram and LinkedIn people who follow you on both platforms may feel that it's redundant to follow you on both and will stop following. You also miss the opportunity to leverage the unique formats of posting that each platform provides. Video and image dimensions, location-based tagging, linking to external content, and even frequency of posting should vary by platform based upon what generates the most engagement. You may post an infographic to LinkedIn on a topic and on Instagram you present that topic as a short video or series of photos in a post. Even staggering the timing between platforms can help increase the frequency of visibility.

Given that each social media site resonates with different people it makes sense to switch things up and alter your approach. Learn through experimentation what works based on which platform to create the most engagement. Using various social networks is ideal for targeting top talent. Below is an overview of how you can optimize your social media strategies to fully tap into the top platforms, such as: LinkedIn, Facebook, Twitter, Instagram, and YouTube. Although we aren't going into detail with many of the other platforms it's important to note that you may want to look at others based upon who you're needing to recruit and where they live. It's important to note that by the time we first print this book one of these platforms could fall out of fashion or be bought by Facebook and mothballed. Do your research to verify the relevance of these platforms. Ask your key staff and candidates about the platforms they're using today.

If you're recruiting in the Middle East, you would need to look at a tool like Telegram. WeChat is the dominant platform for Mandarin speaking people globally. Line is presently the dominant messaging platform in South East Asia. If you're targeting tech orientated staff, you may find that some public Slack Channels or Discord Servers may be great guerrilla recruitment tools. With that said let's take a look at some of the dominant social networking platforms of today:

LINKEDIN

LinkedIn is used by over 87% of recruiters that use social media. It is seen as more of a professional platform than other forms of social media, and it was designed to help professionals connect and facilitate the recruiting process. You can tap into professional groups where there are a lot of people with the skillsets and career interests aligned with your job vacancies. For example, if you're searching for a sales professional, you can post about it in the sales professionals' group. Posts on LinkedIn should be professional and concise. You should continuously update your company's LinkedIn profile to show when you're actively recruiting. Join key professional groups such as the Sales Association to be noticed by members and to engage thought leaders. You can advertise jobs on the site for additional impact. "**Work with us! #XYZCompany #salesjobs #nowhiring**" type posts are highly targeted. LinkedIn has a paid recruiter membership that has a specific suite of tools that are geared specifically to social recruiting.

FACEBOOK

A lot of marketers and recruiters dismiss Facebook as being not a serious platform to do business on or share job opportunities. With over 2.2 billion active users, Facebook remains a highly used platform that is a valuable addition to any recruiter's toolkit. As organizations realize the impact Facebook can have, more professionals are jumping on, currently 55% of recruiters that tap into social media use Facebook. Post descriptions of job openings and include visuals or photos if possible. Use Facebook Messenger to engage potential candidates.

With the Facebook advertising platform, you have multiple ad formats and "goals" to choose from to make your ad campaign a success. For example, you can have a short video showcasing your workplace with an "apply now" button which can then capture critical contact information (name, mobile, and email). Your system can then follow-up via email with a full in-depth application link. You can use Facebook retargeting pixels to show ads to anyone who has visited your site for a specific frequency and period. Many applicants will visit a site and abandon the initial process. Reengaging them increases the odds of people submitting their application. Facebook combined with Eventbrite can be a powerful tool to promote online career fairs.

INSTAGRAM:

Consider the power of tapping into a social site where young professionals engage with others on average 53 minutes per day. Because many young professionals spend much of their time on Instagram, use this space to capitalize on visual messages such as photos and videos that give insight on your corporate culture such as employee recognition events, company charity initiatives, or showcase team achievements. For business accounts there are multiple ad formats and lead capture tools available for advertisers that are specific to Instagram. You can even apply for a job right within the Instagram App if your application is designed to be mobile friendly.

TWITTER

280 characters might not seem like a lot of digital real estate to promote your job opening but 47% of recruiters use Twitter. Tweet a message including a link to a job posting and include hashtags, such as "**Open accounting position with XYZ Company! (link to the job description) #XYZCompany #nowhiring**". Using these hashtags, you have doubled your reach by targeting two groups; anyone following XYZ Company and people searching for jobs. You may want to research popular tags in the regions you're targeting.

Advertising on Twitter is inexpensive, and you can target people based upon region, hashtag, people they follow or tweet about, and even look-alike audiences that are similar to your existing followers. These ad formats can be simple tweets, static images, animated images/GIFs, and explainer videos as well. The advantage to Twitter is that it's the most open-networking platform of all the social platforms. In Twitter search you can search up a topic and comment and/or interact with people posting about that content even if they're a stranger. It's socially acceptable to engage people you don't know and is often encouraged. It is not however advisable to publicly @reply to people with job postings or pitches. Use the art of conversation and engagement to build rapport and then eventually reach out privately with an offer.

YOUTUBE

More than one billion users who watch on average one hour of videos per day on YouTube makes this platform a very intriguing method for recruiters to expand their reach. With videos having the biggest amount of impact in social media, recruiting your company can creatively use YouTube to improve candidate experience, and reduce the time-to-hire by showing, via video, what you value in employees and what makes your company and its employees unique. An excellent example of this is done by consumer goods giant P&G (Procter and Gamble) https://youtu.be/5I3tC_v-nRI

With videos you can capture a day in the life of employees to help candidates picture themselves on your team. Employee testimonials provide insight as to what it's like to work at your company. YouTube videos can help you explain your recruiting process step-by-step by letting candidates know what to expect when they apply for vacancies at your company. This knowledge of the process can help keep candidates engaged. YouTube allows you to livestream events, interviews, and webinars through their platform as well. They are as simple as loading up a regular YouTube video to watch.

KEEP IT PROFESSIONAL

Your public social media accounts should not contain information, personal beliefs, or opinions that are not relevant for potential recruits seeking more insights on the company, its culture, and the job itself. It's important to realize that "keeping it professional" does not mean to keep it overly sanitized. For instance, human rights, equality, and inclusivity are not political issues as much as they are relevant human issues that ideally, are aligned with your organizational values. Taking a stand publicly may prove to be a vital employee retention and attraction side benefit as well – not doing so proactively could brand us as complicit in a myriad of negative social positions. Taking a stand should not be for recruitment or branding purposes. It should be about living and breathing the authentic ethos of your organization.

SEND THEM HOME

When you share a job posting on social media link it back to your company's official social media site and webpage. This provides valuable additional information to potential candidates that wish to learn more about your business. This allows you to track the online journey of potential candidates, increases the chance of you capturing their email contact information, and allows for retargeting them through various ad networks.

A PICTURE SAYS A THOUSAND WORDS

If a picture says a thousand words, then videos must say exponentially more! Video is the medium that social media users are 10 times more likely to engage with than any other form of content. Videos with captioning are the most effective, depending on the social network, up to 80% of viewers will watch videos with the sound turned off. Remember that you carry a full recording studio in your pocket or purse, videos of teammates working, learning together, and socializing to help job seekers visualize being part of the team. This creates excitement and helps applicants develop a greater connection with the company.

POWER OF HASHTAGS

Adding relevant hashtags to posts, which is a method of indexing them, means that anyone who searches that hashtag could easily see your post. So, by sharing a link to a job posting for a graphic designer position, you might include hashtags like #graphicdesigner, #graphicdesignerjobs #graphicdesignerlife or #designerjobs. More widely used generic hashtags include: #jobsearch, #careers, #jobhunt, #employment. #jobposting, #HR, #work, #staffing, #jobopening, and #jobs. The challenge with generic hashtags on platforms like Instagram is that you have a lot more competition for visibility not unlike popular keywords on Google. For Instagram tagging Instagram Stories with #tags can greatly increase their visibility.

FREQUENCY RULES

Social media recruiting is not a "one and done" exercise. It requires the commitment to a minimum of multiple posts per week. Most of the algorithms that determine how many people will see your content in their feed put significant preference on those that post content more than one time daily. Twitter for instance heavily favors those that carry on conversations with multiple active users daily. Frequent postings are not enough, it's critical that daily you respond to messages and comments to build engagement. By keeping up the frequency of posts you create more opportunities to connect with interested candidates, increase your algorithmic ranking, and ultimately increase brand awareness on your chosen platforms.

BE AUTHENTIC AND ALIGNED WITH YOUR BRAND

People are not fooled by fakes, so be authentic, fully aligned with your brand, friendly, entertaining, and professional like-minded people will be drawn towards you. If you make claims that you cannot keep, don't pay proper compensation, onboard employees incorrectly, or your claims diversity fall short of reality – it will show up on the internet quickly and often will permanently negatively impact your brand. It's not about being perfect, it's about being real, and congruent online with our offline reality.

CARING IS SHARING

One of Denis's favorite quotes is by Cavett Roberts, "No one cares how much you know, until they know how much you care." Most of your posts should not be "selling the position" rather, they should be engaging your followers and storytelling. If you invest the time to provide interesting, information, and engaging content that says you care about your online audience they will recognize your efforts by liking and sharing. The more shareable a social media post, the better it will perform and it is highly likely that it will be shared by those that might not be interested in that specific job, there's a good chance there's someone in their network who might be a better fit.

LET'S GET PERSONAL

Potential employees want to get the inside scope and a real sense of what it's like to work at a company. Corporate public social media posts are useful, but they don't provide a story like an employee's posts can. Individual posts are seen as transparent glances into the inner workings of the company and that employee's role. Companies with strong employer brands have the added benefit that because their employees are engaged and happy. Naturally they will share these positive sentiments on their social media accounts. This is often-called organic employee advocacy; the key is to accelerate this natural inkling by providing continual fresh content and tools to easily share them that we mentioned earlier in this chapter. Employee advocacy is the single biggest driver contributing to the recognition of your brand as an employer of choice. This includes letting your teammates know about job postings as they can share these links and their comments to their networks.

EVALUATE WITH KPI'S

Engaging correctly with social media recruiting takes time and effort, it's important to measure and evaluate your results using KPI's. This feedback will quickly show you which efforts are yielding the best results and which need to be adjusted or improved. Great things to measure are the number of people you are reaching, the extent that people are engaging with you, your influence (which people are participating in the conversation and what actions they take), and share of voice (how does the conversation about your company compare to others?). How your social media recruitment impacts time to hire and cost to hire.

One big measurement of your branding and social recruiting efforts is your level of online influence. This seems like an ambiguous term at first but there are many ways we can track our level of influence. The question of course is what makes a brand or an individual influential? Should we look at the follower quality and count of the people they interact with? Possibly the number of important bloggers or LinkedIn influencers that write about them? Or how viral their messages get shared? As guerrilla social media marketer, Jay Levinson, would say you should measure success in profit and net-action or results. Here is the basis for what we consider influential:

John C. Maxwell said it best when he said,

"Leadership is Influence."

He didn't say leadership is a good idea, a vision, or a title, he said influence. Influence can be defined for our purposes as causing someone to take action (internally as in personal growth or externally as in doing something). So, we can imply the following:

Influence = Action

Following are some examples of action that you can measure:

- Message gets passed on
- Number of applicants as a result of social media traffic
- Getting linked to from blog or new site
- Changing or molding views of your audience
- Registering and attending online events
- Solving problems
- Getting feedback
- Listening and creating the brand and it's relationships
- Generating dialogue
- Getting press

- Capturing an e-mail address or contact info
- Acquiring followers or subscribers

There are many more. The important factor here is to go beyond the follower count or celebrity mentality and to realize that authentic engagement that drives real business value is the gold standard, not popularity or trendiness.

Regardless of your sales, business development, or recruiting goals or objectives it all comes down to this formula: Leadership = Influence = High Value Action

AI POWERED RECRUITING

Socially Recruited is a unique AI technology that can reach up to 85% more candidates with the right job ad, by targeting the right social media platform and at the right time. Tapping into AI so your ideal candidates' online activities can be monitored and analyzed means you can best them with the right job ads, on the right sites at the right time to most effectively gain their attention!

> Regardless of your sales, business development, or recruiting goals or objectives it all comes down to this formula: Leadership = Influence = High Value Action

Other forms of AI being used in recruiting are AI driven Chatbots, powered by engines like IBMs Einstein, and loaded up with large question and answer libraries. These bots can converse with potential candidates and escalate conversations with interested and qualified candidates to a live recruiter. There are AI driven email messaging tools that can be programmed to reply, measure engagement, and even book interviews.

ONLINE JOB BOARDS

Online job boards such as Monster, Glassdoor, and Indeed are another vital part of the recruiter's toolkit. Approximately 60% of all job seekers begin their job hunt via online job boards. Denis has been a huge proppant encouraging clients and audiences around the world to adopt online job boards as part of their approach to proactive recruiting. In fact, back in the summer of 2000, he was hired by JobsDB.com (Asia's largest online job board at the time) to do an extensive multi-country speaking tour educating thousands of HR professionals on the merits of this new technology. In North America, he was the keynote speaker at various launches of job boards such as Apprenticeship.com.

According to similarweb.com, Indeed alone gets 424 million visitors per month. Getting onto these high visibility job sites can drastically increase the chances of your advert being seen by your ideal candidates. Consider using niche job boards too, the ones specific to your industry. When seeking tech workers, consider Dice.com, go to GitHub for IT talent, or consider Caterer for tourism and hospitably candidates. Online job boards are either free or affordable ways for your recruiting messages to reach your target audience. Many offer comprehensive paid solutions and allow you to manage large and on-going recruitment efforts with ease and expert's assistance. You can plug these platforms into your in-house applicant tracking systems.

Applicant tracking systems (ATS), which are used by 98% of Fortune 500 Companies offer plenty of benefits, like sorting through candidates, ranking them, and keeping their files for future reference. There are cloud or SaaS based ATS platforms out there for businesses of any size, budget, and industry type.

RECRUITMENT CHANNELS EFFECTIVENESS

As with every investment it is a smart track where you are getting the best bang for buck. Recruiting is no different, it's critical to assess which channels are producing the best results for your business. Some of the most important recruitment metrics that need to be measured for each channel include; quantity and quality of applicants, number of interviewed candidates, cost per hire, time to hire, quality of hire, and employee turnover and attrition. By taking the time to assess each channel a picture will emerge as to the best looking areas to invest your recruiting efforts.

PRE-SCREENING AND INTERVIEWING

PRE-SCREENING USING SOCIAL MEDIA SITES

Given the massive daily usage of social media sites by most of the population, it makes sense to use these platforms as well as Google as part of your pre-screening process. Doing this will help you verify applicant information, as well as provide valuable insights into the candidate's background that might not have been disclosed in their application.

There are multiple reports where a Google search of an applicant uncovered a drunk-driving conviction that appeared in the local crime section of an online community newspaper. If your online application asks, "Have you been convicted of an offense for which no pardon has been granted?" and the applicant says "no" and you later discover that they had made false statements, you have to seriously consider whether this individual is the right person for your team. Employing persons with a past conviction will be an issue for some employers that require bonded employees. In this case, an impaired driving charge may not be an ideal trait of a school bus driver or long-haul trucker. However, it's important to note that many organizations have created programs in partnership with local governments to provide a meaningful career on-ramp for past offenders to become productive and contributing members of society.

In 2018 Career Builder study employers shared leading types of posts and behaviors by potential candidates that raised red flags:

- Posted provocative or inappropriate photographs, videos, or information: 40%
- Posted information about them drinking or using drugs: 36%
- Had discriminatory comments related to race, gender, religion, etc.: 31%
- Was linked to criminal behavior: 30%
- Lied about their qualifications: 27%
- Had poor communication skills: 27%
- Bad-mouthed their previous company or fellow employees: 25%
- Screen name was unprofessional: 22%
- Shared confidential information from previous employers: 20%
- Lied about an absence: 16%
- Posted too frequently: 12%

It is important to remember the old adage, "Validate the messenger before accepting the message." That is to say not everything found online is factual. Misinformation and outright lies are common on the Internet; thus, the recruiter needs to do additional research to get to the truth. A critical component of pre-screening is investing the time to do a thorough reference check.

Recruiters need to be aware of any follow the laws in your region and regarding the type of data you can acquire on a candidate from their social media profiles and other sources online. Note this can vary greatly from jurisdiction to jurisdiction.

Recruiters need to be aware of any follow the laws in your region and regarding the type of data you can acquire on a candidate from their social media profiles and other sources online. Note this can vary greatly from jurisdiction to jurisdiction.

USING AI TO STREAMLINE PRE-SCREENING AND CANDIDATE EXPERIENCE

Unilever, Atlanta Public Schools, Hilton Hotels and Resorts, and nearly 100 other employers now use HireVue, an AI hiring system that uses candidates' computer or mobile cameras to analyze their facial expressions, vocabulary, and changes in their voice. It then compares them against other applicants using an algorithm based "employability" score. Large employers with high volumes of applicants are using AI to help find candidates, assess résumés, work chatbots, and VR to showcase a day in the life of someone doing that specific job. Online skills testing, online personality assessments, and streamline hiring by digitally pre-screening and conducting the first selection interview has been effective for these companies. If a candidate is successful to this stage, they then move on to the second interview conducted by HR employees. Not only can AI improve the efficiency of the pre-screening process but by removing human elements, it eliminates bias and ensures a standardized one-for-all selection process. This helps to ensure the best people get invited to the second interview, which can positively impact diversity in hiring.

Canadian bookstore giant, Indigo, with over 200 locations is a well-respected brand that for years has ranked among the top 10 in Top Retail Employer Brand lists. The company emphasizes on employee experience and enjoys receiving an average of over 2200 online applications every single week. The challenge was that the selection and hiring process was decentralized and this responsibility fell on each store manager. As store managers doubled as hiring managers many issues emerged from the fact that most managers were not trained in pre-screening and they were dropping other priorities such as running the store, focusing on retail results, developing current employees, and special in-store initiatives as a result. Lack of experience and systems resulted in poor candidate experience, delays through the recruitment pipeline, hiring managers missing out on quality talent, cost of vacancies, cost of marginal hires, low engagement levels, stress leave, and loss retail business.

Indigo wanted to use technology to support their immense talent pool and achieve two goals; improve their candidate experience and continue to cultivate their award-winning corporate culture. The solution they opted for was using AI to centralize and streamline recruiting and pre-screening. The results within the first four months of adopting the new system were impressive. Candidate experience was improved as candidate wait times dropped significantly. Automated resume screening processed top candidates were quickly identified and contacted. The process freed up time for store managers that they used for high-value tasks such as face-to-face interviewing and relationship building. Screening costs plummeted 75% and overall cost per hire reduced by 71%. The process reviewed previous applicants and rediscovered quality past candidates and tripled the size of the talent pool. All these improvements to the candidate experience lead to reducing management stress, increased quantity, and quality of candidates, all while freeing up valuable time for the store managers to focus on strategic retail campaigns as well as the learning and development of current staff.

To do this, Indigo used Ideal which is an AI-powered talent screening and matching system which was built to help larger organizations make more accurate, fair, and efficient talent decisions. The AI aspect of course largely reduces mundane and repetitive processes while reducing bias in the hiring process.

We have to remember it's Human Resources not Inhuman Resources, we don't want to automate and dehumanize every aspect of our people recruitment. AI is still evolving and can't screen for values, empathy, leadership, and several other vital selection criteria for today's virtual workforce. Use AI and other technologies that can help make your process better but don't rely too heavily on it for any one aspect of the recruitment and human capital management process.

INTERVIEWING — GETTING TO REALLY KNOW EACH OTHER

Given the global shift to remote teams, companies should be using this opportunity to evaluate their current interview process and to see if any needed changes or tweaks are required. In short, a selection interview is the best opportunity to gauge how well the candidate will fit in with the culture of the organization and to determine if the individual's skillset and key competencies are best suited for the job at hand.

While evaluating your interviewing process it's important to consider the following questions.

- Is it designed to give you the information that you need to accurately determine the best candidate to select from?
- Is it free of any unnecessary barriers or obstacles that are blocking excellent candidates from being considered for the job?
- Does it provide for a good candidate experience, clarity of expectations for the candidate, as well as reinforce your employer branding?
- Is the process structured enough to ensure fairness while still allowing for flexibility to accommodate for a deeper dive into a candidate's experience?

Many people lament that not being able to do real time, in-person interviews reduces the potential of being able to gain insights about the person's personality. In a virtual interview you can quickly establish rapport by starting off with a friendly non-threatening approach.:

- By taking the time to thank the candidate for applying for the position and their interest in being part of your team can get things started on the right foot.
- By using non-threatening close-ended questions such as "did you see the game last night?" or some other conversational opener to get the candidate to relax and open up.

It important that you are looking for facial expressions and body language as the candidate is answering questions. But it's also important to understand that your tone of voice, facial expressions, body language etc. will do a lot to set the tone and atmosphere for the interview. If a collegial approach is fundamental to the culture of your team you should be demonstrating and modeling a friendly approach to your interviewing questions.

Once an initial rapport has been established when it is time to begin a deeper dive into the subject matter. The use of open-ended questions and behavioral based questions is appropriate here. The more detail the answers the more of an opportunity you have to learn valuable insights about your candidate. For example, asking them if they like working on a remote team? Requires a simple yes or no response and doesn't provide much insight, however asking them what they like most about working in a virtual environment and what they like least about working with remote teams can open up a substantial dialogue and provide fascinating insights into what makes this person tick. Behavioral based questions focus on specific skillsets that you would like to see evidence of that you are seeking.

Sometimes it makes sense to do several interviews with potential candidates. The first interview could be with a larger organization with someone from HR who is just doing a quick check in to verify some core competencies and quick values align with the organization. If successful, this candidate then can move onto a second a much more detailed interview with their immediate manager.

Given that collaboration is vital with virtual teams we are seeing a lot of organizations that are using committee-based selection interviews where they have representation from the person's future manager, one or two teammates, and potentially another person or two from other team's departments that they would have to connect with regularly. This 360° perspective offer is valuable insight. Another benefit of this technique is that if the person is hired, they've already met some of the key players which will greatly facilitate their onboarding process.

The type of questions that should be asked should cover areas such as insights to their character, their core values as well as deeper dives into their core competencies to ensure that they have the experiences and the skillsets needed to do the job. Not all candidates may have 100% of exactly what you're looking for, yet you still may wish to proceed and hire them. It is still important as the deep dive questions can identify specific competency gaps that can be addressed very early once a person has been hired through their individualized training and development plan.

When looking to recruit people for virtual team there are multiple great questions that can hone in on the specific area such as:

- What were your biggest challenges you faced in previous remote teams and what did you do to overcome them?

- If they do not have previous remote experience, consider asking them why do you want to work from home?
- How will you be able to stay motivated without an in-person manager?
- How do you schedule and prioritize your work?
- How would you describe your ideal home office set up?
- How would you describe your communication style?
- How do you overcome slumps in personal productivity?
- What is your biggest challenge you face as a remote worker and how do you successfully deal with this?
- What do you think are the key skills necessary to be a successful remote worker and how do you rank yourself on these skills and why?
- What distractions do you typically have? What do you do to ensure that these distractions don't interfere with the quality of your work?
- What are your favorite productivity tools to use and what are your least favorite?
- What are your preferred times to work during the day?
- What does work life balance mean to you? To what extent have you been able to achieve a quality work life balance? What specific things have you done in the past to achieve this work life balance?
- What would you do if you had an urgent question or concern and your team was offline?
- When having to deal with a challenging issue or a difficult conversation with a teammate what process would you use? And what medium would you use?
- What project have you collaborated on that you are particularly proud of and why that is so?

An interesting approach some companies are taking is to create some sort of a task assignment or small project that the candidate is to have fully prepared and ready to present on during the interview. This approach can provide excellent insights to their thinking process is problem-solving abilities and their communication skills as a present back the results.

Some of the danger signals you should watch out for as you're listening to candidates' responses are:

- If the candidate appears to be struggling with an answer through a lack of knowledge about your organization.
- If they have a lack of depth of knowledge relative to a specific skillset that they claim to have.
- Poor communication skills.
- An overall lack of enthusiasm towards the job opportunity for your team and your company.

Upon completion of the interview anyone involved in conducting the interview must take the time to organize their post interview thoughts or notes while it's still fresh in their mind. Does the person fill the job requirements? Do they possess all the core competencies? Will they fit in well with the team and organizational culture?

CHAPTER 4

ENGAGING TODAY'S DIGITAL WARRIORS

A Q1, 2020 study by Doodle says, "Only 16% of HR professionals in the United States said they were prepared to go fully virtual with their recruitment and onboarding programs. Remote meeting tools tend to be low-priority items in HR budgets despite the surge in remote meetings." New employees who were onboarded virtually had a hard time feeling like part of the team and managers struggled with employee engagement and effectively integrating them into the corporate culture according to the study.

ONBOARDING - PULLING OUT THE VIRTUAL RED CARPET

Remote workers have the additional challenge of requiring a fully functional office at their home without the "water cooler" or causal impromptu chat in the hall with a teammate. Given this reality, company's need to empower their people with tools that enable communication and they need to share with the new person when they're expected to be available virtually.

Their employee experience is different from an office worker and it begins with a strong employee onboarding program. Employee onboarding is the process of welcoming recruits and helping them become happy, productive, and fully engaged workers. A new employee's first impression of the job, co-workers, supervisor, and the company will be for the most part developed during the first week on the job. New employees start a job with enthusiasm and positive energy and it is critical to keep this attitude.

Virtual leaders should adopt the mindset of *pulling out the red carpet* by welcoming the new employee to the team. One idiom in sales leadership is that winners want to win quickly; if a new sales pro is hired, is not onboarded quickly, nor ramped up fast, they may quickly lose motivation and leave. Sales winners want to hit the virtual ground running.

A benefit of an effective orientation is that the new employee's decision to join with your company has been reinforced so that they feel that they have made the right decision. This is a smart investment of time to reduce staff turnover. Employee turnover costs employers a tremendous amount of time, energy, and money. It has been identified that the largest proportion of employee turnover occurs in the first 60 days of employment.

The task of onboarding a new virtual teammate should be shared by many in the company. Human Resources should be seen as the support mechanism that helps coordinate all departments in welcoming new hires. Senior executives need to define and model the vision that all staff – especially new employees – are welcomed, supported, encouraged, and developed. Team leaders having the most daily direct contact and communications with their teammates, have a critical role in welcoming, and developing new employees. Teammates play another critical role in the collegial support and connections with their fellow new teammates.

8 MOST COMMON CONCERNS OF NEW REMOTE EMPLOYEES

1. Is this the right job for me?
2. Will I be able to do the job?
3. Will I receive the support that I need, given that I am physically separate from the team?
4. Will I be able to manage work/life balances?
5. Will I fit in and be welcomed?
6. I'm younger/older/or I am from a different cultural background. Will I be understood and respected?
7. The pace here is so busy. Will someone actually be able to take the time to train me?
8. Am I going to be kept in the loop or miss vital company insights and conversations?

Ultimately the new employee's experience boils down to how they felt during the first week on the job. Research by multiple studies shows a strong correlation between a new remote workers emotion during the first week and their overall level of productivity, ability to learn, fitting in with the culture, and developing strong connections with teammates and their manager.

COMMON EMOTIONS FELT BY NEW EMPLOYEES DURING SUCCESSFUL ONBOARDING

- Welcome
- Connected
- Safe
- Important
- Proud
- Happy
- Confident
- Respected

COMMON EMOTIONS FELT BY NEW EMPLOYEES DURING UNSUCCESSFUL ONBOARDING

- Confused
- Disconnected
- Frustrated
- Worried
- Bored
- Nervous
- Afraid
- Upset

Note: If new people experience these negative emotions, they will be on their way to becoming disengaged with their work and the company, which leads to poor levels of productivity and higher rates of turnover which impacts our online brand.

7 COMMON MISTAKES TO AVOID

1. "Mind-Cramming" trying to stuff a week's worth of information into several mind-numbing hours. Make sure your training is broken up into smaller on-line bytes or bites of information. If your initial company onboarding used to be a 90-minute seminar in-person, modularize it, and vary formats. You don't want to try to move it online as is. Instead of a 90-minute Zoom video meeting and a PowerPoint, deliver a 30-minute presentation plus Q&A and then assign the new employees the task of reviewing additional information independently at their own pace.

2. "Make it up as you go" informal and unprepared process. The reality of business today is that everything is at a fast pace. That being said, the notion of "go slower to go faster" applies here. A formal orientation process should be well thought out and should include clear instruction regarding safety and productivity expectations. Care taken at this stage will result in a shorter training cycle, less waste, and increased production.

3. "Like watching paint dry" hours of data dumps, form-filing marathons, and "death by training videos." Today's workforce as mentioned before responds better to smaller bytes/bites of training information that is accessible on-demand and easy to find. On the inexpensive minimum viable solution to build something like this could be a searchable Google Wiki which links to a series of unlisted YouTube videos tutorials made with an iPhone or screen sharing software. On the higher end you can look at training software or platforms solutions such as Trainual, Kitaboo Insight, Bridge, or Ispring Learn to create a more engaging learning environment. Many of these tools have gamification, competency testing, and are all tied to the individual development plan of each employee.

4. "Sink or swim" by throwing a new employee into the fray without support and coaching. Many employers have some form of "buddy system" to assist the recruits. The key to fully capitalizing on a buddy system is to ensure that

the right people are selected as buddies, that they receive training in their roles as buddies, and perhaps most importantly, that they actually want to be a buddy. Sink or swim can happen in many aspects of onboarding. You may train a salesperson well on product knowledge but set them up for failure by not training them effectively on the CRM system or your in-house video conferencing tool. They may need to have multiple internal buddies depending on what competencies, technical knowledge, and processes must learn to do their job well. Someone or something must manage this whole process and check-in to ensure that all aspects are addressed.

5. "No news, is good news", an absence of any feedback to recruits regarding first few days on the job. As stated above it's not enough to have a plan, we must ensure each step is effectively executed. We need to make sure that we are continually assessing and monitoring how effective the overall onboarding plan is and what improvements can be made.

6. "One-size fits all"– dealing with each employee exactly the same way. We need to bear in mind the individual's age, gender, culture, experience, expertise, personality, learning style, and emotional/social intelligence. All of these things need to be taken into account to fully connect with the individual and make them feel 100% welcome. The good news is there shouldn't be a lot of surprises if the pre-screening and selecting processes have been done accurately as you would have a clear understanding of the uniqueness of each recruit and how to best onboard them.

7. "It is not my job" to welcome a new employee. The bottom-line is it's everyone's job to make a new colleague feel welcome and comfortable. This is where we need to collectively demonstrate the organizational values and welcome them to the bigger team. We need to embrace this principle but provide existing employees with an understanding of what type of knowledge, support, or guidance they are expected to provide to new team members.

12 DISCIPLINES OF AN EFFECTIVE EMPLOYEE ONBOARDING PROCESS

1. New employees feel welcomed, valued, and connected.
2. New employees feel proud that they made the right decision to join the company.
3. New employees feel that they are part of the "big picture."
4. Recognition and rewarding of new employees' contributions.
5. Collect and share company stories to make learning points memorable.
6. Make the experience interesting and interactive for new employees.
7. Design the process from the new employees' perspective.
8. Select the most effective time and method of communicating orientation information.
9. Deliver your program in bite sized chunks of information.

10. Have an effective buddy system as part of your orientation program.

11. Get an early evaluation of orientation from new employees and supervisors.

12. Remember, leadership is everything. Ensure that managers, supervisors, and buddies have the needed training for their portion of the onboarding process and they have a positive attitude.

The onboarding process for remote teammates normally consists of the following phases listed below.

- **Recruiting and Pre-screening**. How the new recruit was treated throughout the recruiting, pre-screening, and selection process will set an image in the mind of the recruit to what extent the company lives up to its employer brand.

- **Job Offer and Welcome Package**. Once the job offer has been signed, provide the recruit with the softcopy of a new-hire welcome package which is normally prepared by human resources. This package usually contains items such as employee tax, banking, benefits and legal forms, job contract, job description, company organizational chart, company directory (or a link to it), and an employee handbook (ideally hosted online) with key policies. Using an online documentation resource such as DocuSign or SignNow for delivering and collecting the paperwork is recommended.

- **Create a new employee FAQ**. Use an intranet/wiki page, on your favorite cloud service or create a simple Google Doc. Start by asking new, as well as established employees to submit questions. Add the answers as the questions come in. In a short time you will have created a dynamic resource to answer new employee questions.

- **Create excitement for new employee arrival**. Before the official start date, ask people from the new hire's immediate team why they love working at your company. Email some of the quotes to the new recruit. Ask several future teammates to schedule a virtual coffee meetup with the new employee before thier first day on the job. Have the team leader text or email a brief note explaining why they're excited to have them on the team. Consider asking a senior leader to write a welcome note or record a welcome video.

- **Essential Set-Up**. Before the new employees first day several essential things should be set-up including; login information or passcodes, their email address, group messaging tool, list of key contacts, an itinerary for the first day, scheduling information for the first week, summary of assignments, and goals for the first week.

- **Set up a remote workspace**. To have your new recruit hit the ground running it makes sense to provide them with a list of the equipment and tools. Ensure that your remote employee has the following equipment: phone, computer, printer, webcam, microphone, router, office supplies, desk, and chair. If they're expected to host client webinars or video meetings then other items such as lighting, branded backdrops/greenscreens, sound dampening tools, and additional software. If they're selling a physical product, they may need inventory for promotion and demonstrations.

- **First Day – First Impression**. Make sure that you pre-plan an informal video call with the immediate team to welcome the new employee during the first day. This needs to be done well and scheduled in the first day's agenda as it is one of the most impactful aspects of the onboarding process. Using an UberEATS type service to send lunch to them and immediate teammates provides a casual atmosphere to do introductions over video conferencing.

  Other key things that can be done during the first day are: a morning video chat with their leader to welcome them, answer any outstanding questions, provide a virtual office tour, introduce them to their buddy, and discuss goals and assignments. **Assignments and goals** should have been shared before the first day of work, but now it's **time to discuss those items in depth with KPI's while giving the employee a chance to ask questions and add goals that excite them**.

- **First Week – Getting Acquainted and Building Relationships**. Consider having your new teammate work from your office so they can further develop the relationship with their teammates. Virtual coffee chats with various teammates is a great way to help the new employee connect with others and fit in with the team. Involve them in multiple projects so they get the chance early to work with multiple teammates and immerse them in important work. Offer recognition for completed tasks and accomplished goals.

- **First 30 Days – Settling In and Avoiding** "Hires Regret." It's critical to not let communications drop so we highly recommend having one-on-one meetings weekly to keep on top of projects, provide performance feedback, continue on-going mentoring, and reinforce the professional relationship. Organize virtual team building sessions with the entire team.

- First 3 Months – Adjusting and Becoming Fully Engaged. Measure to determine if the remote employee is happy and satisfied with an engagement survey and obtain feedback on every aspect of the new employee's onboarding experience and make any needed improvements.

Documents on a shared folder or an outdated static wiki or spreadsheet just aren't enough to manage the onboarding process effectively, especially if you're experiencing growth across multiple divisions in your company. Platforms like Bamboo HR, NewWired, Sapling, EnBorder, and Ultimate Software are just some of the tools you can use to manage the onboarding process while creating an engaging and productive new employee experience. It's important to note that these tools do more than just help with onboarding, Ultimate Software for instance is a complete Human Capital Management solution which manages the employee's entire lifecycle experience from their first day as a candidate to their exit interview.

TRAINING AND DEVELOPMENT, THE BEST INVESTMENT IS THE INVESTMENT IN YOUR PEOPLE

Imagine if you could increase employee productivity by 50% to 200%, would you be keen to learn how? This is one of those "no-brainer" questions as everyone would say "yes". The next logical concern would be how incredibly expensive or difficult it would be to make that kind of improvement? In reality it is not very expensive or challenging to get these types of gains in productivity. All it takes is the effective training and development of your employees.

According to the **Association for Talent Development (ATD)**, "Companies that offer comprehensive training programs have up to 218% higher income per employee than companies without internal training. These companies have 24% higher profit margins than those who spend less on training."

Research by Dale Carnegie shows that companies with engaged employees outperform those without by up to 202% and that 40% of employees will quit their job if they don't receive adequate job training within the first year.

A recent study by **Capgemini Consulting**, says, "Only 10% of U.S. workers feel that they have sufficient computer and Internet skills to use the digital tools they need to fully do their jobs." With the rapid rate of technological change that we referenced several times throughout this book, it's imperative for employees to receive continuous learning to remain relevant.

With the above statistics the value of training and development and its impact on productivity becomes clear. Leaders of virtual teams state that remote employee training and development can be challenging.

COMMONLY CITED CHALLENGES OF REMOTE TRAINING AND SOLUTIONS

- **The lack of in-person presence** has many leaders and trainers concerned that the learners can't be monitored will lack commitment to learning and that their attention will wander. If you communicate the importance and value of the training, while keeping the training session concise, your employees will be motivated and committed to the training.
- **The lack of access to information about the training**. The solution is to provide each learner in advance the following information; training overview, learning objectives, key outcomes expected, who is it targeted for, how long is it, when is it, what advance preparation is required, how and where to access the training, and how to get help if required.
- **The lack of social interaction**. This is one of the areas that remote learning shines as it provides a great social connecting opportunity for remote participants to get to know each other and the trainer while answering questions and participating in group discussions.
- **Lack of focus**. Distractions can be a factor for remote workers, however if the employee is aware of the time of the training, they can take the needed steps to minimize disruptions. For instance, if you're leading a sales team don't schedule training near month-end or during critical sales and client hours.
- **Lack of problem-free training**. It is virtually impossible to guarantee that there will be no technical challenges despite your best efforts, however the following section provides a few ideas to minimize any hiccups.

BEST PRACTICES FOR VIRTUAL TRAINING

Selecting the right training tools can be as simple as emailing notes in advance and sharing to a small team via Facetime. Secondly, you could use a conferencing tool like Zoom to share your PowerPoint presentation, poll the group, chat via text, access each other files, and record the session. The third option could be a professional eLearning platform like GoToTraining that would have many more features specifically tailored to running training like, quizzes, conversations, simulations, case studies, virtual assessments, and breakout classrooms for group work.

Before selecting the training tools, it is recommended to first ask yourself the following questions;

- What are the learning objectives/outcomes that the training is designed to provide?
- Who are the target learners?
- How will we test and track learning results?
- How much time is allocated for this training?
- What is the training budget?
- Is this a one-off training session or will this training need to be delivered to many other people/ groups?
- What training method (presentation, role play, case studies, group discussion, videos, etc.) would be best to accomplish this?"

BEFORE DELIVERY OF TRAINING

Once you have answered these questions you will be able to select the right training tools. Based upon the training tools selected you will be next able to build your training content. Remember when it comes to online training, less is more. An hour or two of highly engaging and impactful learning yields better results than forcing people to endure 8 hours of mind-numbing information overload. Creating an enticing agenda for your training shows participants "what's in it for them" so they are keen to take your training. Include any pre-training prep or materials that your learners will need in advance of the session. Break your training up into smaller groups and schedule it at different times of the week to increase engagement and ensure everyone attends, while having enough staff to complete critical tasks. Before starting the training go through the checklist provided below to ensure that you are fully prepared and everything works well.

DURING TRAINING

Although there are many things that could be discussed here, we will cover the most important. First of all, stick to your training schedule. One of the fastest ways to lose learners is by rambling off topic and going past the allocated time. Doing so portrays the image that you are not organized, professional, nor care about the learner's time.

By factoring in some discussion time into the agenda you can cover interesting points or questions as they arise and still respect the agenda. Before jumping into the meat of the topic it is best to do some sort of icebreaker, a fun exercise, or ask each participant what they hope to learn as a result of the training.

Ultimately you want to fully engage all of your learners and one of the best ways to do that is to appeal to all three learning styles. The three learning styles are auditory, visual, and kinesthetic. The best way to appeal to auditory learners is for the trainer to use their voice (changing tone, volume, pitch, and speed) to tell interesting stories that reinforce the principles being covered. Visual learners greatly appreciate PowerPoint slides, charts, graphs, photos, and videos embedded as part of the training. While kinesthetic learners are very tactile and they respond best to training that is supported by exercises, roles play, and other hands-on learning. Regardless of the trainers preferred style of learning (that will reflect in their nature style of teaching) trainers need to become comfortable with easily and often transitioning from each of the learning styles throughout the training session. It's important that we learn with all of our senses, regardless of what our dominant learning style is, a training program that engages all the senses creates full association, stimulating, and improving retention and implementation.

Ebooks and audible books are great ways for staff to access non-fiction material that progressive companies are now providing budgets to pay for, and encourage ongoing learning and development. Some teams have even organized regular book clubs through video conferencing to discuss their views and what they learned from each book. Extending the topic beyond work specific can deepen and broaden the context of employee relationships. Learning about mindfulness, or something fun like a wine appreciation course, or the important history of local Indigenous communities can bring staff together through meaningful conversations on topics that are not traditionally thought of as being work related.

Walkme.com is a platform that provides on-the-job employee training in a short and simple process to complete tasks effectively, without the need for prior knowledge. This site helps companies and their employees accelerate Digital Adoption by delivering -by-step guidance through a sequence of tip balloons without requiring the user to leave the screen, watch video tutorials, read manuals, or FAQ pages.

VIRTUAL MENTORING

A mentor cares about the mentee's long-term success and commits to assist in the "fast- tracking" of the person's development. This is done by the mentor sharing all of the lessons that they themselves have learned over the years. This form of compressed learning can shave off years of learning for the mentee. The mentee to get full value out of this relationship must be "teachable" and open to this relationship dynamic. The mentor must have credibility alongside the title of boss or leader. In fact, the mentor doesn't have to be a boss and may be a colleague. A teachable person is someone who is enthusiastic about developing him or herself and is open to learning new things.

Companies that have mentoring programs enjoy greater productivity in the workplace. Employees that head the advice received from their mentors learn quicker, are more productive, and make less errors, which all drive real results. Mentee's commonly state that they greatly value the relationship with their mentor all of which positively impacts engagement. Mentoring programs attract greater quantity and quality job applicants.

BECOMING AN EFFECTIVE M.E.N.T.O.R.

The M.E.N.T.O.R. acronym outlines the key competencies, attitudes, and behaviors of a great mentor:

Models success

Expands Vision

Navigates

Truthseeker

Optimizes

Relationship Building

M – MODELS SUCCESS

Great mentors model success. Authenticity and transparency are much sought after but rarely found characteristics in today's society. People listen to what we say as mentors but we have to be cognizant of the fact that we tell a story about what we truly value by our actions and daily disciplines.

Mentorship provides a pillar and a model of possibility for those who follow us. Our example of success and constant movement forward is what makes us credible and creates an environment of faith where the mentee feels safe to take risks and move outside of their comfort zone. This is true of anyone who is mentoring a team going through a massive change involving technology or new economic realities. The mentor must lead the charge and demonstrate through their actions a willingness to embrace and constantly learn about new technology and its applications.

Another important trait of modeling success is that we too need mentors to help us continue to grow. After all, it's pretty difficult to follow our lead if we're no longer moving.

E – EXPANDS VISION

As a mentor our path to success often gives a 20,000 foot view of the market and business environment – this gives us insight and vision, because of the distance we have traveled we can naturally see further and more. Great mentors often help formulate and paint a bigger picture than people can conceive on their own. The mentor's conviction in the vision and belief in the mentee fuels the faith and conviction that the mentee needs to spurn them forward. Great mentors expand their mentees, vision, self-concept, and standards consistently. Spend time teaching people how to think bigger and set goals that seem slightly out of their grasp.

N - NAVIGATES

The ability to navigate and provide a proven strategy for success is what people look for in a great mentor. The feeling as a mentor to be able to give this gift is fantastic. Navigation has three components, a destination, a place to start, and as a mentor we provide the third ingredient – the path in between. People will always have unexpected obstacles during their journey but it's the fork in the road that shows the true value of a mentor.

T - TRUTHSEEKER

Truthseeker. A mentor isn't there to coach or counsel someone. There is no fee, rarely a contract, and the only reward is often the reward of legacy, contribution, and mentee transformation. The mentor relationship is a transformational one where we focus on helping someone reach and become their full potential. In navigation we talk about needing a starting point. Great mentors through relationship development can peel away the layers of persona to find the person, and the truth of the situation. The truth of any situation is where we can begin to map a path forward. They help the mentee develop clarity and evaluate murky situations to find the real truth and reality to build life and business strategies that are based upon accurate assumptions and wise choices. Transformation can only truly begin with a truthful beginning. Seek and insist on the truth.

O - OPTIMIZES

Optimizing is about taking something that is already effective and improving it significantly by making a series of subtle calculated shifts. Transformation rarely happens all at once. It usually occurs through a series of smaller changes and shifts in focus. As a mentor when we work and develop others we can see a hundred things they could improve. Optimization is about prioritizing based upon strengths and talents. Help your mentee delegate or remove the activities and behaviors outside of their core talents and values. Get them to focus on what they are truly good at and what they truly enjoy doing. On purpose people have more energy, hardly feel stressed, and are more productive.

R - RELATIONSHIP BUILDING

Relationship building is the key to having real impact and leverage in the mentorship relationship. Through relationships we gain the trust of the person, once they trust us deep truths, fears, and goals are shared. We gain permission to give them much needed feedback and direction. We have all been in the situation where someone offers advice to us when uninvited, we can feel that this person is assumptive and pushy, and more often than that we don't feel that the advice is credible after all we hardly know the person.

Shane's late father, Bill Gibson, was a mentor to both of us in our speaking careers and lives. One of the legacies he left us are his teachings. He developed a very straightforward formula for relationship development.

Time + Genuine Assistance = Relationship = a commitment from both parties.

There is no shortcut here, the more time we put in and the greater the assistance and positive intent the stronger the relationship and ultimately the better the results.

We can genuinely assist people in many ways; we can:

> **Time + Genuine Assistance = Relationship = a commitment from both parties.**

- Believe in them
- Help pick them up when they have failed
- Commend them when they have succeeded
- Help expand their network
- Make them part of a project you are working on
- Recognize them publicly
- Keep commitments

Another critical component of building relationships and effective mentorship is listening. Listening seems simple enough but most people don't, they just wait for their turn to talk. People spend a good portion of their day being talked at and competing for airtime. People can tell when we truly care about them and what they have to say. Authentically listen to people, be totally present and sincerely interested, and the relationship will flourish.

Every conversation a mentor has with their mentee makes an impact, thus it is critical to build rapport early in the relationship. This will establish a needed level of trust between both people by not only talking about work but by also discussing their goals and other facets of their life. It is recommended that a validated personality assessment tool be conducted on the mentee so that the mentor has a better understanding of the personality style of the other person and this knowledge will provide powerful communications insights.

Make sure both the mentor and mentee understand what each wants and expects from the mentoring relationship. Before starting the mentoring, relationship be clear about how much time can be allocated per session, and how often. Confirm which video conference tool will be used for the main mentoring sessions and which tools will be used to communicate between sessions.

During the one-on-one mentoring sessions allow enough time for the employee to provide updates and discuss concerns and for you to properly cover the topics you have identified. At the core of every successful mentoring relationship is the honoring of commitments, if something is agreed upon, do it.

It's critical that both parties take the mentoring relationship seriously and come prepared for each session. Avoid canceling mentoring meetings as it conveys that the other person and the relationship is not your priority, reschedule it if you must.

When mentoring remote workers, it's important to maintain frequent points of contact, otherwise the old adage holds true, "out of sight, out of mind." By checking in regularly with text, email, social media messages or calls, both parties will remain engaged, and committed to the relationship.

In the work environment mentors are frequently managers or senior managers in the mentee's organization. For mentors it means they are often wearing more than one hat at a time. Mentorship in a work environment is often about grooming and preparing the mentee to grow into a larger role within the organization. Part of this process is optimizing performance and giving mentees a toolkit for person growth. To get the best results, we encourage the Socratic Method, essentially don't give them the answers, instead facilitate them discovering the answers themselves. Following is our 5-step process to performance improvement leveraging the mentorship relationship.

FIVE STEPS TO IMPROVE PERFORMANCE USING A MENTORING APPROACH

1. Create a relationship with your mentee.

    - Identify any emotional triggers or listening blocks that would interfere with your effective listening.
    - Have a questioning process or check-in method to get them talking.
    - Find the right time to raise the issue.
    - Demonstrate genuine interest and belief in the mentee.
    - Use an inviting and encouraging tone of voice.

2. Present the opportunity for performance improvement.

    - Start by reinforcing a positive by pointing out a specific accomplishment or success.
    - Encourage them to offer up areas for growth or opportunities for improvement.
    - Be clear and direct about what the performance redirection issue is.
    - Limit the statement to a single issue (not a whole litany).
    - Use objective, positive, and professional language, without judging or blaming.
    - Emphasize the wish to resolve the issue (redirect behavior) positively.
    - Indicate belief in the mentee's abilities, including his or her ability to resolve issues.

3. Listen for the mentee's perspective.

    - Listen actively to understand the mentee's perspective.
    - Paraphrase and use open-ended clarifying questions.
    - Acknowledge the mentee's perspective.

4. Resolve the issue with your mentee.

    - Maintain a focus on work-related behaviors.
    - Seek to get input and solutions generated by the mentee.
    - Reach mutual agreement on the nature of the problem.

- Collaboratively develop strategies and timelines together to address the growth opportunity.
- Move towards wrapping up by reinforcing a positive; pointing out a specific accomplishment or success.

5. Get commitment on action steps.
- Get commitments for specific, time based, measurable action steps.
- Follow up on all commitments.

The following is a pre-meeting prep-sheet to help mentors be effective and impactful during their time with their mentees.

MENTOR'S PRE-MEETING PREP-SHEET

Meeting Date___/___/___ Meeting Time _____ Meeting Platform _____

Mentee's Name _____ Previous Meeting Date ___/___/___

Prepare for a mentoring session by reviewing the points below.

Explore any follow-ups from the previous meeting.
Discuss mentee's recent "successes" which you have noted.
Explore mentee's SMART goal(s) they have achieved or are on track to achieve.
Explore mentee's SMART goal(s) that they are no longer on track to achieve.
What specific job-related competencies do my mentee need to develop?

Ask what challenges or obstacles are they facing now? Offer your observations on this.
Seek mentee's suggestions to overcome these challenges or obstacles. Offer your ideas.
Obtain specific actions that mentee commits to and will be held accountable for by the next meeting ___/___/___?

PUT THE FOCUS ON PERFORMANCE

Everyone wants feedback; human beings crave it. Consider the various recreational activities we pursue outside of work; whether it's sports, online video games, or a board game, we all keep score. The score is direct feedback of how well we played. We all want feedback, especially positive feedback when dissevered plus insights on how to get better.

One of the challenges of a workplace is that sometimes the only time we get feedback from our supervisors is when something has gone wrong. One of the cautions we give clients is not to get involved in "Peek-a-boo management." This is a management style in which supervisors keep a low profile, spying on their employees until somebody messes up, and they can spring a "Caught you" on them. In the virtual work environment this could manifest itself as over-using tech to micromanage people. Tech tools should be used to manage performance and not make employees feel that every keystroke or email is being monitored in real-time.

Employees are seeking feedback linked to growth. According to research by The Robert Walters Group, 91% of millennials consider career development the number one priority in their jobs. They want frequent, formal feedback on a monthly, or at least a quarterly basis to help them continuously improve their skills and performance. They want continuous just-in-time informal feedback as well. It's important to note that although Millennials may be the most vocal about these needs most people in the workforce respond favorably to this type of management environment. Gallup recently found that "only 20% of employees say their performance is managed in a way that motivates them to do outstanding work, and only 14% feel that their performance reviews inspired them to improve."

One of the single biggest challenges cited by virtual leaders is the feeling of being disconnected with their teammates. They feel it is challenging to observe both the strengths and the challenges of their direct reports. Without physically being there to interact with them, observe the behaviors, actions, and tasks of their staff they feel that it's difficult to gauge and provide performance feedback.

That being said there are ways through ongoing communication plus the assessing of actual output and results that can provide virtual leaders with the critical information that they need to accurately gauge performance. By doing so this ensures that poor performance doesn't go unchecked and become a dangerous habit and that effective and positive performance gets noticed and recognized. This will encourage more of the same positive behaviors while adding to the level of engagement and satisfaction of the employee while driving real results for the business.

Best Practices to Evaluate Virtual Workers Performance

- Don't worry about the number of hours worked, instead focus on evaluating the quality and quantity of work and tangible results achieved.
- Stick to the facts by focusing on data not opinions.
- Don't wait for the once or twice annual formal performance appraisal session, instead hold weekly meetings with remote employees that define tasks with deadlines.
- Establish KPIs on productivity, willingness to raise their hands to work on new projects, collaboration with others for remote employees, and measure their outcomes based on these metrics.
- Seek internal feedback from the employee's teammates to get a fuller and more accurate picture of the individuals' areas of strength and opportunities for development.
- Evaluate the soft skills like professional ethics, teamwork, proactiveness, self-motivation, collaboration, problem solving, and emotional intelligence among others that are essential when working virtually.
- Use focused one-on-one video-based performance feedback and mentoring sessions monthly (weekly if possible) to track your remote employees' performance. You learn a lot through facial expression and body language about someone's mental state and outlook that might not be evident with just an email or even phone call.
- Train all managers with new tools, techniques, and platforms to improve performance management and the use of empathy to increase virtual team motivation and achievements.
- Create a learning and developing culture where everyone sees on-going performance reviews as a positive and is something that enthusiastically committed to.
- Follow the **70/30 Rule** which states that leaders should limit their talking to 30% of the time during performance feedback sessions so that they can listen for 70% of the time and thus learn insights from their employee.
- Use performance improvement feedback that is "sandwiched" between two layers of praise. This makes people more receptive to your constructive comments and ideas and more open to committing to improvement.

It's critical to introduce and reinforce a performance management process with your remote teams to create a strong, constant feedback loop while focusing on increasing the quality and quantity of communication within your team that drives results. It's important to revisit what we mentioned earlier in regard to digital platforms and tools. The on-going support and communications needed for mentorship and performance management is most effective when you leverage the right digital tools.

You no longer have the lunchroom, watercooler, or even the bench outside the office to have informal conversations. These conversations added up over time are just as vital if not more than formal mentoring and feedback sessions. You build this informal communications channel into your digital environment with tools like Microsoft Teams, Slack, Discord, and Salesforce Chatter – they enable impromptu quick casual interactions and social connection opportunities.

EMPLOYEE RECOGNITION

Companies that have invested the time and energy to build a culture of employee recognition enjoy stronger engagement, increased employee morale, better customer service, and lower turnover. Acknowledging achievement is such a simple and inexpensive thing to do yet it can increase productivity by 50% higher and drive real bottom line results by 20%. Leaders are not the only people that should recognize employees, but fellow teammates should acknowledge their peers as well. It is interesting to note that often peer recognition has more of a positive impact on financial results than manager-only recognition. The goal for virtual leaders is to create a culture of recognition by empowering all teammates to recognize their peers, direct reports, and managers.

Look up the words *recognize or recognition* in any dictionary and you will find definitions that use words such as "see", "identify", and "acknowledge". These words are at the core of what effective employee recognition is about. Employee recognition means management cares enough to take the time to see, identify, and acknowledge the organizational contributions, valued behaviors, and good efforts of employees. Recognition is an essential element to any successful working relationship. Employees must know that their work matters and is important to the company and teammates.

As individuals, not all people value the same recognition for similar activities or behaviors. Personalizing the recognition process is the most effective way to motivate and increase performance, develop employee skill, acknowledge, contribute, and meet organizational objectives.

12 BENEFITS OF EMPLOYEE RECOGNITION FOR EMPLOYERS

- Motivates employees by acknowledging their achievements.
- Enhances an individual's self-worth and self-confidence.
- Reinforces positive behaviors to both individual and entire team.
- Positive virtual team reinforces employers' brand, draws passive job seekers, and increases likelihood of employee referrals.
- Reduces employee turnover and absenteeism.
- Fosters a sense of pride in work and company.
- Enhances relationship between supervisors and workers.
- Promotes positive open communications.
- Creates loyal employees.
- Improves productivity.

- Reinforces company culture, values, and aligns desired behaviors with company goals.
- Increases profits.

Recognition does not have to cost a lot of money. All it takes is a bit of creativity and innovation tailored to the needs of your virtual teammates. By doing the following activities regularly you will be on the fast-track to developing a rewards and recognition culture.

Seven simple steps to rewarding and recognizing employees:

1. Consider how you might like to be thanked for your efforts.
2. Ask them what type of reward they would appreciate.
3. Praise publicly and criticize privately.
4. Develop the habit of looking for reasons to praise people, it will raise the bar.
5. Identify the specific positive behavior or performance being acknowledged.
6. Reward/ recognize positive performance as soon as possible to reinforce behavior.
7. Make the process fun and engaging.

BUILDING AN EMPLOYEE RECOGNITION PROGRAM

As stated before, it is critical to start by building a culture of recognition that reflects the organization's values and business strategy. The program needs to be defined and communicated across the company. It works best and is more readily accepted when employees are involved in design and implementation of the program. It's important to maintain creativity and fun while providing a mix of formal and informal programs. To avoid stagnation, programs need to change periodically.

Building a timely and specific recognition program is more meaningful when supported with educational tools and when the reward is personalized to the individual.

The characteristics of effective recognition are:

- **Timely** – as soon as possible after the positive achievement
- **Proportional** – matches the action in type and degree of recognition
- **Specific** – identifies the positive behavior and positive impact to company
- **Individual** – recognizes the person involved
- **Sincere** – comes from the heart and shows you care
- **Personal** – reflects the unique personality and interests of the recipient

THREE KEYS TO EFFECTIVE EMPLOYEE RECOGNITION

1. Invest Time

To engage employees, consider making time for personal talk such as enjoying coffee together over a Zoom call periodically or making time to inquire about their life outside of work. When you make time to show interest in a fellow employee, you are demonstrating recognition for the individual. Employees are more likely to share their interests, challenges, and successes if they feel that you are genuinely interested in what they have to say. Showing interest and engaging employees will be a zero cost yet effective way to begin a relationship and to provide meaningful individual recognition.

2. Determine what is Important

Know what is important to employees, at work, and outside of work. Recognition encompasses accepting each other as unique individuals and acknowledging that each of us has a life outside of work. This will enable a better understanding of employees, their values, and how you can demonstrate recognition effectively on an individual basis. To make recognition a valuable and meaningful tool, it is essential to determine what is important or perceived as valuable from an individual perspective. This is where being connected on platforms beyond LinkedIn becomes valuable. For instance, being active on Instagram and following your team on that platform leaders share their personal side, hobbies, and interests while learning more about their team and their lives. Depending on your team demographic and interests you could be connecting with them on Tik Tok or even gaming with them. The casual conversations in the backchannels of social networks can often help us learn a lot about people.

3. Individualize

Finally, break into the core of recognition. Find out specifically when, what, and how employees like to be recognized. Having employees who feel valued is an essential step to creating a healthy and positive workplace and enhancing performance. Employees who feel valued are likely to have increased performance, decreased absenteeism and turnover rates, and may be able to influence the morale of other employees in a healthy and positive way. When providing recognition at a personal level - keep it simple! Be spontaneous yet sincere. Start to take note and comment on the things that are valued by that individual.

ESSENTIAL ELEMENTS OF RECOGNITION

- Match the recognition to the person according to what is important to them.
- Link recognition to performance and real results of the company.
- Be timely by giving recognition as soon as possible after desired behavior.
- Always state why recognition is given to ensure clarity and repeat behavior.
- Make it fair by allowing all employees equal opportunities for recognition.
- Switch it up and think outside the box for creative recognition ideas.
- Involve your team in determining what recognition they value.
- Praise publicly, provide constructive improvement feedback privately.
- Remember the two most powerful words, "Thank You."

SOME IDEAS ON HOW TO RECOGNIZE REMOTE WORKERS

- Send lunch via Uber eats type service to the employee with video conferencing chat over lunch with a senior leader for a casual talk and mentoring.
- Send dinner to an employee's immediate family to thank them for all the extra effort their loved one has put in.

- Use social media to recognize employees for their special efforts. Use visuals and tell in story format why this person deserves the shout out. LinkedIn for instance has a special feature when posting where you can select to write a special recognition or thank-you post for someone you work with.
- Peers can send other teammates public bonuses that can be easily redeemed for a wide variety of gift cards, donations, and other prizes via tools like Bonusly, a rewards and recognition platform.
- Share a brief article on your company website showcasing several top employees.
- Send a unique experience such as; riding a hot air balloon, Italian cooking lessons, or a caricature sketch of a wedding or vacation photo all depending on the interests of the employee being recognized. Blueboard is a platform where your employee chooses their desired experience (based on budget inputs set by management) where their concierge team takes care of all the logistics to create a meaningful experience.
- Take the time to ask an employee or survey the team to find out what they might like as a potential reward, normally it will be not what you would have guessed. If the budget is reasonable why not give them what they want.
- End each week by hosting a "Crushed-It" video meeting with your team and have each team member say who on the team "crushed it" that week and why.
- Present a plush bulldog animal for your most persistent employee.
- Consider giving a spark plug award and gift certificate for the brightest idea within the previous month.
- Tap into a simple yet powerful "thank-you message" with Reward Gateway, an employee engagement platform, which delivers customized e-thank-you cards through its peer-to-peer recognition program.

WITH NO TRUST THERE IS NO VIRTUAL TEAM

Trust is at the core of every functioning team, simply stated **where there is no trust there is no team!** Trust, although it requires time and energy to build is so worth the effort as it fosters collaboration, enhances relationships, reduces silos, expands teamwork, enables change, and drives engagement. In a recent online article in Inc. Justin Barisol shares, "Google recently set out on a quest to figure out what makes a team successful. They code-named the study Project Aristotle, a tribute to the philosopher's famous quote "The whole is greater than the sum of its parts." The results according to Google: "In a team with a high level of trust, teammates feel safe to take risks around their team members. They feel confident that no one on the team will embarrass or punish anyone else for admitting a mistake, asking a question, or offering a new idea."

Researchers at the Center for Creative Leadership state, "When trust is present, people step forward and do their best work, together, efficiently. They align around a common purpose, take risks, think out of the box, have each other's backs, and communicate openly and honestly. When trust is absent, people jockey for position, hoard information, play it safe, and talk about— rather than to—one another."

In a recent US study, researchers found that compared with people at low-trust companies, **people at high-trust companies reported:**

- 74% less stress
- 50% higher productivity
- 106% more energy at work
- 13% fewer sick days
- 76% more engagement
- 29% more satisfaction in their lives
- 40% less burnout

12 INDICATORS OF LOW TRUST THAT VIRTUAL TEAMS LEADERS MUST WATCH OUT FOR

1. Every conversation is strictly business with lack of personal connections.
2. "Us vs Them" mindset and emergence of protective silos.
3. Everyone out for themselves focusing on their needs and agendas.
4. Team members "bashing "each other.
5. People reluctant to ask or offer assistance.
6. Communication breakdowns and lack of information sharing.
7. No one owns up to their mistakes.
8. Micromanagement by the virtual leader suggesting they don't trust their people.
9. Negative people undermining morale.
10. Unresolved conflicts that escalate and cause resentment or even hostility.
11. Team members not delivering on commitments.
12. Low levels of engagement, productivity, and missed deadlines.

Building and maintaining trust as we have said before is the foundation of every meaningful relationship however it can be more challenging in a virtual environment given the physical distance and the reality that some teammates have never actually met. Although it is every teammates responsibility to positively contribute to the enhancement of trust within the team it is critical that the virtual team leader sets the stage for building trust within their team. To get a better understanding of the key characteristics required by leaders of virtual teams to build trust please complete the following self-assessment.

VIRTUAL LEADER TRUST BUILDING ASSESSMENT

For each statement, place an "X" to rate your teammates on a scale of 1-5 where:
1 = Strongly disagree 2 = Disagree 3 = Neutral 4 = Agree 5 = Strongly agree

Virtual Leader Trust Building Behaviors	1	2	3	4	5
I believe that my teammates have the team's best interests in mind.					
I believe that my teammates are capable at their jobs.					
I have faith in the abilities of my teammates.					

Virtual Leader Trust Building Behaviors	1	2	3	4	5
I lead by example, I walk my talk, and this includes technology use.					
I communicate honestly, directly, and transparently.					
I admit my mistakes and acknowledge my limitations openly.					
I keep my promises and commitments.					
I trust my people and I believe in them.					
I ask for feedback and accept it gracefully.					
I don't play favorites or use double standards.					
I use the same standards, expectations, and treat everyone fairly.					
I never start or spread gossip.					
I listen more than I speak.					
My actions, behaviors and moods remain consistent.					
I put the success of the team before my own.					
I never throw a teammate under the bus.					
Virtual Leader Trust Building Score:					

STRATEGIES FOR BUILDING TRUST

The good news is that there are multiple strategies that virtual leaders can use to build trust. Many of these strategies are indicated in the Virtual Leader Trust Building Assessment above. Although there is no pass or fail mark with this self-assessment it is important to note that any characteristic scored below a "4" is an area that we recommend to be closely examined and changes be quickly made to the behavior so it is in-line with the ideal score of "5".

DON'T TUNE OUT CONFLICT

Some degree of conflict within any group of humans is normal, the challenge is to minimize conflict. Although this can be harder for virtual managers it is vital in your role that you keep a pulse on your team and encourage everyone to communicate often to avoid misunderstandings. Despite our best effort's misunderstandings do occur, when this happens don't delay, and wait for things to fester and eventually blow up. Conflict doesn't naturally resolve itself. Take action immediately and nip it in the bud and try to avoid taking the easy way out by sending a text or email, instead picking up the phone do a video chat. It will be more personal and effective. There's a much higher chance of being misunderstood in a text or email than a video or phone call.

EMBRACING CULTURAL DIFFERENCES

Part of a dynamic organization is having a diverse team. Leaders need to be able to anticipate and account for cultural differences across the team. The more geographically spread out your team is the more you need to foster a truly inclusive environment.

Diversity and inclusion must be built into the organization's culture from the very beginning as a cornerstone to establishing real trust amongst teammates.

A recent McKinsey Global Institute study "Delivering Through Diversity" found that:

- Gender-diverse organizations' financial performance is 15% better
- Ethnically diverse organizations' financial performance is 35% better
- For every 10% increase in diversity on executive teams, organizations saw an 8% increase in profitability

THE POWER OF FACE-TO-FACE TIME

Regardless of how well you tap into technology to leverage communications it is important for your team to come together several times a year to do team building exercises, brainstorm, do strategic planning while deepening personal connections if at all possible.

SPECIFIC WAYS TO USE TECH TO BUILD TRUST IN VIRTUAL TEAMS

Companies can use Slack real-time communications to keep their virtual teams connected while streamlining workflow through the use of channels that help teammates organize all of their conversations.

Virtual teams can use email systems that are transparent and keep everyone in the loop by allowing each employee to see their teammates' emails. Various email lists are created for specific teams or projects that way everyone that needs to receive a specific gets it while eliminating unnecessary email flooding others' inboxes.

Google's G Suite provides budget-friendly options to encourage employee's collaboration. Google Forms can be used to keep an idea log that can be shared with teammates. Ideas can be presented via Google Slides and Google Sites is an option to create an internal wiki. Gmail is another tool that offers advanced filter options and labeling that can be used to block irrelevant messages and optimally organize conversations.

Zoho CRM has a great add-on tool called Zoho Connect, it is a team collaboration software that simplifies communication and streamlines processes that facilitates employees communicating and builds trust amongst each other, asking questions, posting helpful information for others to see, and brainstorming.

Virtual teams that want to communicate about projects and see their progress can use project management software like Trello. This type of software simplifies collaboration and employees feel a greater sense of accountability as they see how their output impacts others and they can better manage their deadlines.

An example of a business using tech to build trust through transparency is online training company SI Certs. They used Slack and created a channel titled #revenue and integrated their payment platform, Stripe. Every time a sale is processed by Stripe, it shows up as a notification on their channel and employees can see the company's revenue growth in real time. This real-time, transparent approach drives performance in that when the team's numbers are down everyone immediately knows and can resolve it, when revenues are up people immediately get the feedback that their efforts are paying off.

In short, the greater level of team engagement the higher the performance and their willingness to stay, play, and be part of your team. As a virtual leader, you need to embrace and leverage some of the dozens of platforms we have covered in this chapter. It's about creating multiple channels for frequent, authentic formal, and informal communications.

EMPLOYEE RETENTION HIRING STATISTICS

- 40% of candidates say they've experienced a lack of communication between when they accepted a job and their first day of work. (G2.com)
- 56% of companies have paid for employees to get skills-based training outside the office, so they can move up to a higher-skill job within their organization. (G2.com)
- The top reasons given by employees for leaving their jobs include lack of career development (22%), lack of support with work-life balance (12%), their manager's behavior (11%), unsatisfactory compensation and benefits (9%), and poor well-being (9%). (G2.com)
- Employee burnout accounts for up to 50% of workforce turnover. (Paycor)
- Only 12% of employees agree that their company does a good job of onboarding new employees. (Zety.com)

In Denis's book *Strategic Talent Management - How to Boost Your Profits in a Disruptive Economy* he describes his **HR/Talent Management Model** and how to maximize the return on investment in all human capital investments. The following model illustrates how this works. When looking at the digital transformation for your human capital management and HR/TM functions it is vital that you look at what pain point issues you have. That is to say what problems or missed opportunities are you facing and then take the time to determine which particular software platform(s) you will need to resolve the issue.

DR. CAUVIER'S PROFIT MODEL FOR MAXIMIZING ROI IN HR/TM/HCM

P– Problem/ Profit Opportunity identification

The first step in any solution is to identify the problem (sales, staff turnover, productivity, union grievances, missed marketing opportunities, rate of absenteeism, wastage, downtime of equipment, accidents, and profitability).

R - Resources wasted (cost of problem)

While identifying the problem is important, the context of the problem must be described if the actual cost to the company is to be estimated. The greater the erosion of the bottom-line or the missed opportunity, the more urgently the problem needs to be addressed.

O – Opportunity for a Solution

This is where leaders have the opportunity to create, purchase, or subscribe to specific software solution(s) to address pressing problems.

F - Financial investment required

This step is the determination of the financial investment that will be required to resolve the problem. This is a critical step, because it provides the all-important "where the rubber hits the road" check to make sure the software solution is not more expensive than the problem.

I - Improvement generated

This step of the PROFIT model calculates the actual dollar amount of improvements directly generated by the software solution over a predetermined period.

T - Tracked ROI

This final step is the all-important measurement of the return on investment. It indicates in a ratio format how much money was saved or generated as a direct result of implementing the software solution. The higher the ratio, the better the ROI, the more real results on the bottom line.

There are many thousands of HR/TM/HCM software platforms and apps out there. In the past most companies implemented a core HR software system (HRMS, payroll, and benefits administration) and then over time added various talent management systems (performance management, learning and development, and engagement systems) on top of it. Now, savvy businesses understand that employee experiences have the most impact on results, retention, and the employer brand as we discussed earlier. It is not enough to have HR platforms that are user friendly; they also have to automate, simplify, and enrich employee experiences. Furthermore, workplace technology and HR technology platforms need to play nice with each other and be able to seamlessly integrate.

To help make some sense of the array of choices we have identified some of the most popular solutions for each stage of the employee E.X.P.E.R.I.E.N.C.E. Although this is not an all-encompassing list it will provide a solid start for your digital transformation process.

HR, HCM, AND TM PLATFORMS THAT DRIVE EMPLOYEE E.X.P.E.R.I.E.N.C.E.S TM CHART

Entering (Onboarding)	Zenefits Goco Bamboo HR Bamboo Sapling EnBorder
X Exiting	Qualtrics Checkster ExitPro
Performance management and feedback	Cornerstone Saba SAP -Success Factors
Engagement levels	Kazoo 15five Reward Gateway
Recruitment process	BambooHR Paycorp Eddy
Individual development plan and mentoring	Tovuti GoToTraining Bridge Trainual WalkMe
Employee referrals and advocacy	Erin Drafted RolePoint
Networking/ Collaborations with colleagues	Slack Office 365 Trello Zoom Webex GotoMeeting
Communications with leader	Facebook –workplace Flock Office Chat
Equity, Inclusion, and Diversity	Jopwell Fairygodboss Textio

When considering which platform(s) to invest in, here are some questions leaders should consider;

- How user friendly is this system?
- Can it be customized to our unique needs?
- Is it practical for day-to- day work?

- Does it reinforce the corporate culture that is aligned with our core values, mission, and vision?
- Is it flexible enough and does it facilitate the adaptation to rapid changes in our working models?
- Does it enable the company to become truly client centric?
- Does it enable us to tap into gig, seasonal, or part-time workers who want non-traditional working terms?
- Does it facilitate hiring, promoting, and paying people in fair, unbiased, and transparent ways?
- Does it support our commitment to diversity, inclusion, fairness, and transparency?
- Does it drive productivity by reducing workplace clutter and distractions so employees can focus on work?
- Does it enable us to adapt our pay and reward practices to be more competitive?
- Does it support our efforts to encourage and support our employee's wellbeing?
- Does it support the planned career path planning, continuous learning, and succession planning of our key and hard to replace talent?
- Does it help assess, identify, and develop future leaders?
- Does it improve the morale, performance, outcomes of virtual, and hybrid teams?
- Does it drive real results in terms of profits?
- What support is provided to help implement and support the adoption of the platform?
- How compatible is it with my existing systems?
- What is the projected ROI (within what timeframe) if we proceed with this platform?

Later in chapter 9 of this book we will offer some additional recommendations on how you can pick a tech advisor (if you need the assistance of one) to help select, implement, and manage the right software for your business's unique requirements and get on the fast track to your digital transformation.

Creating a powerful virtual team doesn't amount to anything if it doesn't lead to real sales. The digital-first thinking and culture that you have created as a result of adopting and

> **Creating a powerful virtual team doesn't amount to anything if it doesn't lead to real sales.**

implementing the tactics and strategies covered so far in this book are essential for your the stage, however, to put things into practice we need to:

- Discover and capitalize on the 13 Big Trends that are changing the way we sell.
- Equip your virtual sales team for success with the right tools and competencies.
- Build a strong virtual brand by using social networks, platforms, and

- Shift to a Digital-first sales and sales enablement strategy.
- Leverage remote meetings, social prospecting, CRM use, automation, and AI, personal thought leadership.
- Select the right sales technologies to help you drive real results and scale in a virtual economy.

The next 6 chapters will help you build your sales, branding, and technology roadmap so that you can successfully put these key strategies into action.

CHAPTER 5

WELCOME TO THE DIGITAL-FIRST SALES REALITY

*"Change happens in an instant.
It just takes us awhile to adjust."*

When Stephen Jagger and Shane released *Sociable! How Social Media is Turning Sales and Marketing Upside Down*, the world was very early into the trend of the democratization of communications. The Yellow Pages and Faxing were still a thing. It was 2009, and Twitter and Facebook were measuring members in the tens of millions. At that time those numbers were already daunting, and the platforms presented a unique opportunity for individuals and brands to use guerrilla marketing techniques to compete against the big guys and gain market share.

Stephen and Shane made bold declarations, such as predicting that the majority of major newspapers would go out of business, and that we all should burn our business cards because no one's going to need them. They were selling the vision pretty hard and believed wholeheartedly that social media marketing and social communications were going to completely change the way we do business.

They were wrong about many predictions, but not in the way you would think. Social and digital communications have become significantly more important to organizational and individual success than they truly thought was possible. With 2.5 billion active people on Facebook and close to 750 million on LinkedIn, social media communications literally touch anyone on the planet who possesses a smartphone or has access to a Wi-Fi connection. A lot of these changes have also been invisible: Amazon, for instance, has replaced millions of retail brick-and-mortar sales jobs over the past decade.

The groundwork for a digital-first virtual economy has been laid over the past 15 years. From tech leaders to venture capitalists to visionary politicians, authors, and thought-leaders there's been a very large cohort of believers who have been preaching the gospel of technology interconnectedness and the always-on Internet-everywhere movement. Most industries, however, were only dipping their toes in the shallow end of the pool, rather than fully embracing the opportunity that digital and social communications provides.

Some trends are gaining momentum in the marketplace that directly impact how we're going to strategically sell and market moving forward. We've identified 13 of them that we feel are vital to take into account if you are going to be a truly virtual sales and marketing organization:

13 BIG SALES TRENDS FOR A VIRTUAL SALES ENVIRONMENT

1. **Client engagement is now primarily digital**: As mentioned previously, the pandemic forced millions of people to work remotely. Many organizations and decision makers were surprised to find remote and hybrid remote work to be efficient and add to the quality of life of their work routine. Most buyers and decision-makers now start their search for suppliers and partners on the internet. They spend many hours a day there, and your presence is not optional if you want their mindshare and wallet share.

2. **You don't have face to face IRL (in-real-life) as a differentiator**: In the recent past if you were a local printer or service provider you had an advantage over someone 10 miles away. Now that we're all virtual, that advantage is less important. In fact, many of our new competitors may not be 10 miles away; they might be in another country and able to deliver solutions virtually just as well as us or even better. This presents us with an opportunity to go global by tapping into major platforms and networks.

3. **More screen time for business and personal (which is good and bad)**: Everyone is now within arms' reach of at least three screens at any time. We're spending more time in front of the screen in meetings, networking, shopping, and accessing our entertainment. If you can actually connect with somebody, they are often ready to virtually interact as they are already online. The downside of this, of course, is their bandwidth for meetings or to consume information is more splintered and limited than ever.

4. **Ecommerce is now the primary channel**: From March 2020 to August 2020 ecommerce had the same amount of growth it'd had in the previous 10 years. According to Canada Post, it was literally Christmas volumes every day. Ecommerce now directly and indirectly drives over 70% of retail sales. To be visible and engage our customers we need to leverage ecommerce platforms. Even traditional retailers have dedicated on-site ecommerce staff who are focused on curbside pickup, returns, and various aspects of logistics. Your local grocery store is now becoming a distribution hub. Even if you're in the service business, it is vital that you ask yourself, "How can I be an ecommerce company that delivers a service product?" rather than the more typical, "How can I add ecommerce to my service business?" Find ways to productize what you do and leverage ecommerce networks and channels.

5. **Instant meetings (are a huge opportunity and expectation)**: As we connect with people instantly and they enter our sales funnel there's an expectation that we can instantly meet with them on a video call or text chat to answer their questions in real time. This is providing sales organizations with an incredible opportunity to shorten their sales cycle, but if they're not able to instantly respond to connect with customers, those customers will go find someone else almost instantly.

6. **Instant messaging**: A recent in-depth study on chatbots found that the majority of consumers would prefer to interact with the chatbot online to have their questions answered instead of dealing with a human. Additionally, most people prefer a text over a phone call, or at least, a text to book a phone call. This shift in preference is something we need to leverage by embracing instant messaging tools and channels - whether it's texting via telephone, WhatsApp, Facebook Messenger, chatbots, or direct messaging through Twitter, LinkedIn, or Instagram. Your customer is now spending as much time in messaging apps as they are scrolling through content on social networks. Sales and marketing are now a conversation and those conversations are happening within chat and Messenger environments. Done correctly, chat and text conversations can be great tools for establishing rapport and sharing the right information with clients, customers, and prospects.

7. **Frequent communication**: Nick Usborne is an expert on writing content for the web. He refers to small easy to consume pieces of content as "popcorn content." As business communicators, we need to become fluent in this style of communication. Because people are constantly inundated with content interactions, questions, status updates, and any other number of digital distractions and interruptions, their attention is fragmented. It's important that we maintain consistent presence to maintain relevance and mindshare. Today's environment has created the need for us to be frequent communicators, providing popcorn content that can be easily consumed and keeps us top of mind, while not bogging down our prospect or customer with gratuitous amounts of text, video, or reports. We need to stay top of mind but also need to make it easy for people to consume our content. It's important to note that our content still has to be valuable even if it's brief and easy to consume.

8. **Mobile First (Smartphones are how most execs see your content)**: Most senior executives will read your email on their mobile device before they look at it on their desktop device. From a retail perspective, the majority of consumers research a product using their mobile device. According to Facebook, the average person scrolls over 300 feet of content on their mobile device daily. People are living on their mobile devices first and this means that our digital-first strategy has to be a mobile-first strategy. Our marketing and sales activities have to take this into account. The way we communicate must be easily engaged with on a mobile device. Mobile devices are driving hyperlocal marketing opportunities, allowing businesses to target individuals of specific interests in real-time in their target market areas. It's important to note that because this

highly relevant and contextualized advertising and marketing is happening, your customer is now beginning to expect it. They don't want a generic ad; they want a relevant ad delivered to them at the right time at the right place, or you become irrelevant and soon you become unsubscribed or muted.

9. **Remote is here to stay**: In a recent poll on LinkedIn by Gary Vaynerchuk of Vaynermedia only 8% of the 3120 people polled stated that they expect to be at the office full time in the near future, 27% intend to work at home mainly, and another 64% expected to work a hybrid of that spending part of the time at work and part of the time at home or working while on the road and remote. Numerous other studies from research giants such as Forrester Research share similar sentiments from both senior executives and their frontline staff. As we indicated in Chapter 1, organizations have realized significant efficiencies by going virtual, and what was once temporary is now becoming permanent for many organizations, or at least individuals within those organizations. This is because their jobs can largely be done remotely while still letting them be effective team members. This is important to us as marketers and sales professionals because we need to now adapt our approach to marketing and communications so that is relevant to the remote decision maker and worker.

10. **Everyone is a media company**: We have 13-year-old kids who have developed incredible branding capabilities, are adept at hosting live video chats, and are wizards at effectively and quickly engaging comments, questions, and community members online. This is the future. It's happening right now. Most people spend several hours a week curating their image online and publishing content. From a business perspective your company and any customer-facing individual in that company must be proficient at online communications.

We are all now in the media game, and we are literally competing for attention with our business rivals next door, corporations on the other side of the world, and the entertainment value that that 13-year-old kid provides the audience. All of these people and organizations are competing for the attention of our potential and existing customers, and we need to build media competency so that we can rise above the noise and engage our target market. Being a media company means investing in the skills and tools to broadcast and engage on multiple channels.

Today it means being good at hosting Zoom meetings, leveraging Instagram stories, publishing podcasts, and doing LinkedIn live video - tomorrow it may involve immersive Virtual and Augmented Reality streaming from your GoPro.

11. **If you're alive, you're in tech**. To maintain relevance and a competitive edge it's not enough to just use technology within our business. We need to start thinking like tech companies, building products, and solutions that at their core are driven by technology. In the past an organization may have been a training company delivering training services. Today they need to be a platform that connects educators and their content in real time with individuals and companies that want to access that learning whenever and on whatever device they prefer to use. It's not

just about putting a trainer in front of a screen anymore; it's about realizing that you're now a technology platform that is ecommerce-enabled, which happens to deliver training content. This business model that we're describing has more in common with ecommerce companies than it does with a traditional educational institution. It needs to think like an ecommerce company first, not an educational company that is using technology to deliver courses. Tesla, of course, is another great example of a market disruptor. When Elon Musk built the company, he focused on building a technology platform that just happened to enable automobiles.

12. **Sentiment shifts are rapid**: The "always on connected to everyone" trend that we're living through has enabled the rise of rapid sentiment shifts. Someone can become a superstar overnight on YouTube, say one wrong thing that offends a certain crowd and literally be "cancelled" by the community that helped build their brand and their connections instantly. Sentiment shifts around even what makes good content, and what got us here from a marketing or communication perspective isn't necessarily going to get us where we want to be tomorrow. We have to invest significant time keeping an eye on where the trends are and realize that no matter what we're banking on today for business marketing results, we're going to have to shift that strategy quickly and on an ongoing basis. It's important to note that although it's painful at the time, that negative sentiment will shift quickly as the crowd moves on to something else. As a brand leader you still live your core corporate values and authentic self, but you have to be aware and nimble so that you can respond to and capitalize on important sentiment shifts.

13. **Digital fatigue and addiction are on the rise**: There have been numerous recent studies on what's been called "zoom fatigue." People who normally were spending a third of their workday in front of the computer are now spending 85% or more of their labor time in front of a screen. This doesn't include their own web surfing or mobile device use. People are burning out and most won't know it until it's too late.

This digital fatigue can manifest in different ways: not being able to concentrate, the inability to get creative, a feeling of emotional exhaustion or edginess, a drop in the ability to maintain concentration, and a lack of patience in general. There are many other symptoms for this digital fatigue, but it's important to note that it's a real and relevant issue that as a leader you need to keep in mind.

If you're leading a team, it's important that you limit their screen time at work, or at least give them good breaks and analog activities to refresh the mind. It's about creating healthy boundaries for your team; this means not texting them after hours just because you had a creative thought, for instance. It's about allowing them to turn off digitally in the evenings or the weekends and encouraging them to set healthy boundaries with their clients as well.

Having your staff always on will give you some short-term gains, but in the long term will result in burnout, a drop in productivity, and employee turnover.

Digital addiction is the next level of the phenomenon of digital burn-out. People have become addicted to hormonal and endorphin highs driven by digital interactions. Many people become flooded with dopamine just anticipating what that little red status update might mean. Constantly going back to your phone to check status updates has been proven to be almost addictive as casino slot machines and equally hard to kick. While it's important to leverage and embrace this exciting world of the digital-first virtual economy, it's important to remember that we ourselves are actually not robots. We require exercise, sleep, real in-person interactions, and time spent in nature or at least outdoors. Consequently, when you're developing your digital sales strategy for your team or yourself, you need to be thinking about developing a strategy that is sustainable and healthy over the long term.

These 13 trends have essentially created an entirely new sales and marketing environment. New environments require new thinking, new processes, and different talents than our traditional offline sales and marketing environments. This next section of the chapter digs further into some of these shifts and how they're impacting sales and marketing. We look at some of the key competencies required of sales professionals and sales leaders that are integral to drive real results in this virtual economy.

Until recently most sales organizations were using the same old-school sales processes. It typically starts with a cold-call or some sort of traditional networking; this is followed up with a qualifying or discovery call, and in many cases an in-person meeting and follow-up to close the deal. The idea of making the sales process digital usually involved the digital bookend. This bookend would look like prospecting on LinkedIn, followed by the same sales process they have always used, or maybe a video call jammed in the middle of the old process. Most organizations in the business to business space, especially those that sell capital equipment or large system solutions, have historically depended greatly on in-person meetings at industry conferences, networking events, and the like. Another important element for many has been schmoozing with clients at restaurants, baseball, and football games, and all the other trappings of large enterprise sales. Even if they were strictly business, most salespeople were road warriors visiting client sites and networking in the field.

Although the ability to remotely and effectively sell and service clients and grow our revenue base has existed for many years, only a small percentage of organizations embraced it. Sadly, most who embraced it saw it as a secondary or tertiary method of connecting with their client base in comparison to the high investment and high touch in-person engagement.

LETTING THE PROVERBIAL GENIE OUT OF THE BOTTLE

The pandemic forced everyone to go remote instantly. Entire demographic groups who were resistant to change had no choice - they had to go digital if they wanted to access the products and services they were dependent upon as individuals or businesses.

The great thing for business is that due to decades of investment in remote management, sales, and marketing tools, most of the needed tools and platforms were available but underutilized. A good example is Zoom video conferencing; they went from 10,000,000 users (which took them close to five years to build) to 300 million users in a period of 11 weeks. Platforms like LinkedIn and Netflix both doubled their monthly user growth over a five-month period. Most of these platforms have become more affordable and more user-friendly than they were even a year ago.

What's interesting about these shifts is that once your customer or client base moves online and discovers the convenience of delivery to their front door, or the efficiency of doing video-based meetings or engaging vendors through platforms, it's more difficult to get them back offline than it was to get them to move online.

This is an important perspective when thinking about the digital-first sales and marketing environment of today. We have heard many sales leaders make declarations around the fact that they're going to bring their sales teams back into cubicles and out into their cars driving the miles to meet clients face to face just like they used to as soon as things go "back to normal".

The challenge with this thinking is that your customers and clients don't care about what you're going to do with your sales team and sales process. What matters to them is their buying process and their preferred methods of communication and procurement. That method is now digital-first for most, especially commercial or enterprise size accounts.

When a C-level executive discovers that they can procure goods and services just as easily through online web conferences or a digital platform as they could previously through multiple face to face meetings, they begin to question the logic of devoting more time, money, and energy to these types of meetings.

Instead of flying people in from other parts of the country to make a major decision and collaborate with the vendor, they can do it digitally. This saves them thousands of dollars and in many cases hundreds of people hours. This becomes an important area of focus.

> **Digital-first sales organizations are customer-first sales organizations. It's not about what we want to do with our sales organization as much as how we're going to align with the new buyer in the digital-first sales environment. It's not about us.**

Digital-first sales organizations are customer-first sales organizations. It's not about what we want to do with our sales organization as much as how we're going to align with the new buyer in the digital-first sales environment. It's not about us.

Most customers have now discovered the incredible benefits of procuring products and services and communicating with their vendors through digital means. They are not going back to "normal".

REMOTE SELLING IS VALIDATED

Even a year ago most executives were skeptical of how efficient their salespeople could be selling remotely. They preferred to keep them within arm's reach. This enabled them to micromanage their daily activities to make sure they stay on track. Out of fairness, a lot of us salespeople are easily distracted, have a history of cutting corners or taking long lunch breaks, and some truly aren't efficient unless held accountable almost on a daily basis. In a digital world, there is no future for salespeople who can't keep themselves accountable to their goals and KPIs.

During the pandemic a shift took place; salespeople were no longer measured by their minute-by-minute activity, their visibility in the office, or the number of calls they even made. They were accountable instead for their results. Many sales leaders discovered that their sales teams were highly motivated and capable of generating results as remote or work-from-home salespeople. They seized the opportunities that independence and remote work offered. Many salespeople we have interviewed and talked to have said this was an opportunity to prove that they could do their job remotely and meet or exceed management and customer expectations. Many lobbied to stay remote after they could go back to the office, citing increased productivity and work/life balance. For the teams that had to be whittled down due to budget constraints or shrinking client bases, it was those that did not adopt the new virtual digital-first sales environment that were the first to go.

Even in the Enterprise IT space many sales organizations are hiring proactive virtual salespeople and are laying off tenured large account managers who were used to meeting in-person, networking, and to some degree farming existing accounts or markets. They weren't able or willing to make the shift to the new, proactive virtual sales reality.

Having worked with several large national organizations helping them shift their selling to digital and social has helped us identify some of the key attributes of successful sales professionals and organizations. We recognized some common steps in the process of rapidly transitioning to a virtual sales culture. Now we're going to share with you these key attributes, competencies, and processes.

THE VIRTUAL SALES WARRIOR

Putting in the miles used to be a rite of passage for sales professionals. The outside sales executive was responsible for chasing down key accounts and covering large territories, bringing home both fat paychecks and legendary stories of economic conquests. We called these sales professionals road warriors. The road warrior has now been replaced by the virtual sales warrior. These two sales archetypes share some similar characteristics, best practices, and competencies, but there are multiple unique attitudes, behaviors, and areas of expertise that the virtual sales warrior needs to acquire to succeed. It's important as sales leaders to be able to identify this virtual sales warrior competency map, so that they can recruit those who already possess this skillset or have the capacity to acquire it.

The virtual sales professional competency map includes all of the traditional sales competencies, plus an entire additional layer of digital sales competencies. Sometimes the way things used to be will get in the way of what works now. Trying to take an existing sales process that worked offline and transition it word-for-word, minute-for-minute, meeting-for-meeting into a digital environment simply won't work.

Shane and the team at the World Trade Centre in Vancouver discovered this running their trade export training programs. The first time they took an offline event and transitioned it online they simply used the same agenda, same speakers, same types of interactions, and expected to get much the same results. What they discovered is that you need to think about the tools available to you and how to use them best to deliver learning rather than just trying to put an offline learning model online. The program went well, but the ratings and the energy of the group were definitely waning.

The next time they delivered a program online they completely reworked the delivery. They took full days and made them half days, 30-minute speeches got whittled down to 15-minute speeches with 15 minutes of Q&A, interaction, and real-time polling. They shifted the curriculum to be less dense and gave attendees more take away material and resources to dig deeper into the topics later on their own.

These shifts resulted in a significant increase in sustained engagement and higher ratings from all attendees. They discovered that a virtual environment dictated a completely different set of competencies from the organizers, AV team, presenters, curriculum developers, and the marketing and logistics team. What made them good at offline events actually didn't necessarily make them great at online events, mostly because they attempted to do it the way they had always done it, instead of starting off studying existing best practices for online conferences.

This story is important because sales organizations are doing this. Their past experience and success are getting and will get in their way when they try to use digital tools and platforms to access, engage, land, and grow accounts.

We experienced this with many clients, years ago as they shifted from direct mail (print mail drops) to email, and even more so from email to tools like Facebook Messenger, Drift, or WhatsApp to connect with customers.

Most organizations' first instinct was to cut and paste a message that would typically be written from a direct mail perspective into an email and send it, but the tone was wrong for the digital medium.

The same thing is happening as organizations begin to use Messenger, SMS, or WhatsApp as channels of communications. They expect to be able to cut and paste or write messages much like you would in an email, and that doesn't work for the medium. It needs to flow like a normal text message exchange: brief, back-and-forth, less formal, and don't forget the emojis ☺.

Most fail at first because they don't notice what works on the platform and what their market responds to or prefers. Instead they just cut and paste an email into LinkedIn private messages and wonder why no one is responding to their generic message.

There's a good chance that the email marketing expert in your office is not the right person to build you a conversations, chat, and text conversations library or strategy. Unless they work hard to overcome their biases around what works in email, they will fail miserably. You have to look at what's working and preferred method of engagement for your target market, and look at where that market is heading in the near future.

Instead of asking what you could do digitally that will replace a coffee with the customer or a lunch meeting, you need to ask, "What highly engaging digital tools are available that will assist in driving engagement and deepening relationships with customers?" These are two very different questions. The first is asking what digital tool can replicate what you're doing offline. The second question asks what digital tools networks and platforms are available to successfully engage your customers. This is the essence of digital-first: what works or what could work on the digital plane. Your experience is likely exactly what is holding you back.

To navigate this landscape and succeed as a virtual sales warrior you need a different set of competencies. Following are the key competencies of a virtual sales professional:

SALES MASTERY

☐ **Master of the basic selling skills**: Basic selling skills cover the ability to quickly gain rapport, ask probing questions, handle objections, present features and benefits, and of course write proposals and then negotiate before closing the deal.

☐ **Mastery of relationship selling skills**: This sales skillset is more about building long term relationships and multiple relationships with clients.

☐ **Mastery of large complex and long sales cycle selling skills**: Long sales cycle and complex selling is about the ability to get by in a group of people within a large enterprise or organization.

☐ **Technology competencies**: These competencies are about the ability to use the core software and technologies available and learn new sales technologies as needed. This can include CRM, hardware, cloud-based inventory systems, or point of sale systems.

SOCIAL NETWORKING

☐ **Content creation**: This skill is about effectively creating content that will be published on social networks relevant to your target market on an ongoing basis.

☐ **Content curation**: Finding great content that resonates with your audience and sharing it. This may be reports, studies, how-to's, or even relevant breaking news.

☐ **Conversational**: Sales and marketing is now an online conversation. This skill is about being able to initiate and respond to online conversations with potential and existing customers.

TECHNOLOGY FLUENCY

☐ **Speaks in tech**: Being able to speak in tech means that the salesperson understands the jargon and core aspects of relevant technologies and is able to interact with technical staff or clients in regard to various technologies.

- ☐ **Data interpretation**: Sales professionals need to be able to interpret data and use it effectively to determine how well their business unit is doing and to present relevant arguments or concepts to clients based upon important data.
- ☐ **Systems and process design**: Great virtual salespeople are design and process thinkers. They can optimize step by step processes and then template them using technology, such as sales workflow tools.
- ☐ **A proactive and curious problem solver**: Technology has its hiccups and great virtual salespeople can figure out how to solve these problems. They can figure out how to connect a new software to their existing system without having to go to technical staff for every little shift or challenge.
- ☐ **Understands the sales tech stack**: For each step in the sales process there are dozens of software solutions that can help with automation. It's important that sales professionals understand how to use these tools within the sales tech stack you have built for them.
- ☐ **Capable of assessing tech tools**: A lot of great solutions and innovative uses of technologies will come from your curious frontline sales team members. The ability to find and assess new technology tools is a great asset.
- ☐ **Learn new programs and tools**: This is about the ability and desire to continually learn about new tech tools, programs, and apps that will help you keep up with the competition or even give you an edge.

VIRTUAL COMMUNICATIONS

- ☐ **Information dissemination**: This is the ability to effectively share information through multiple channels. This means mastering everything from email to text to internal chat tools connected to your CRM. It's about understanding how to present that information in these various channels so that it is noticed and read.
- ☐ **Digital broadcast capacity**: Everyone is now a media company. Today's virtual sales leaders need to be competent and comfortable in front of a camera and microphone. They must be proficient in current leading webinar and video broadcast platforms.
- ☐ **Multiformat, multi-screen, multiplatform writing skills**: Each platform and method of communicating online has a slightly different tone and format that must be followed. Texting, email, and various forms of instant messaging and chat all have their social norms, formats, and cadences that need to be observed to be most effective.

VIRTUAL SOFT SKILLS AND COGNITIVE SKILLS (RIGHT-BRAIN SALES SKILLS)

- ☐ **Trendspotting**: Virtual salespeople know how to get noticed. Part of this is understanding where the action and the conversations are. This is often driven by trends. This will dictate a lot of their content creation, curation, conversations, and where they do their prospecting. Trends tend to be where the customer is focused and where you can gain the most visibility.

- **Pop culture and business culture awareness**: Understanding the pop culture trends, icons, and news, as well as popular business trends and cultural shifts can help savvy virtual salespeople establish rapport and commonalities with their target market in their online and offline conversations.
- **Research skills**: The ability to research potential and existing clients online is immensely important. Being able to sift through hundreds or thousands of web pages, determine which ones are most relevant and then pull up the data that will help you sell and service clients better is key to succeeding in a digital realm.
- **Collaboration**: Collaboration happens a little bit differently with remote teams and requires a remote collaboration skillset. It still requires a team-oriented, collaborative individual to leverage these tools efficiently.
- **EQ/SI (Emotional and Social Intelligence)**: Empathy, self-awareness, and the ability to read other people and understand how to most effectively respond is a key skillset. EQ and SI have a significant impact on a person's resilience and openness to change.
- **Dynamic thinking**: Dynamic, creative, and responsive thinking is vital. This is about multi-faceted thinking, the ability to be a truly well-rounded communications leader and a team member who is equipped to be dynamic in their approach, communication style, or method of selling when needed.
- **Right-brain sales skills**: These are all the skills that can't be automated or effectively imitated by artificial intelligence. They are skills that can make people invaluable to their organization and their clients. In the following pages we will be digging deeper into these right-brain sales skills.

Today's virtual sales professional is truly a technology enthusiast that happens to sell as well. They speak tech and they are using artificial intelligence and automation tools in everyday life. Technology should come naturally to them and your virtual sales rep of today and the near future will require all the above competencies, skills, and behaviors. The final competency of "Right-brain sales skills" will be a key differentiator for salespeople and sales organizations moving forward. This is such an important element of future-proofing your sales organization; we have devoted most of the next chapter to tackling this important framework.

CHAPTER 6

THE RIGHT-BRAIN SALES PROFESSIONAL

Right-brain sales skills and competencies can make a sales professional indispensable and give a sales organization the edge. They may be using the exact same types of technology but if everyone is using the same tech, then that tech is no longer an advantage. The advantage will be in hiring the right sales professionals to work in parallel with these sales technologies.

It's important to note that technology is a tool, not a process. Everyone is in a rush to fall in love with technology, but we forget that we should be working on falling in love with the process that brings us customers first. Buying is still a human activity; it's a personal and emotional process for many of your customers. You need to use technology to help enhance this very right-brained, creative, and emotional experience, not remove emotion nor sterilize and template the experience.

When we talk to sales professionals about future-proofing their careers, our advice is to make themselves indispensable. The way they become indispensable is to truly immerse themselves in the sales technologies that can help give them an edge. Secondly, they need skills that can't be easily automated by computers or quickly learned by competitors.

The right-brained sales revolution has been happening for quite a while. It's evolving to a point where we see a divergence in the sales space. Sales roles in inbound sales, SDR's (Sales Development Reps), call center salespeople, chat salespeople, and the like are becoming minimized and focused in their activities. You need fewer sales skills to do these jobs because many of them are equipped to succeed using technology and are focused on a piece of the sales process versus all elements of the sales process. At the same time large accounts, enterprise salespeople, and business development executives are earning more than ever.

A recent infographic published on Saleshacker.com attempted to visually show the sales tech landscape. It itemized over 700 sales technology companies that cater to sales organizations—there are close to another 5000 companies and sales technology apps out there. These cloud-based SaaS (Software as a Service) tools help automate, streamline, and refine almost every aspect of the sales and customer success process.

For instance, some of these tools can go onto the web in an automated fashion: find people on Twitter or LinkedIn talking about topics that you're interested in, pull their information into your CRM and send an email, call them, or reach out on LinkedIn. Most promise to fully automate and standardize your sales results and activities. The challenge is that many sales organizations are looking for a silver bullet when they implement one of these solutions. It's about exciting new tech that is going to change their entire sales process and do their work for them. The question is how much of their process can be outsourced and automated before the sales professionals become less valuable on the balance sheet or to their customers.

A big part of this trend is the evolution of artificial intelligence or AI. Stephen Jagger and Michael Stephenson are the co-founders of Addy, a blockchain-based real estate micro-investment platform. A few years back they developed a product called IMRE which is an artificial intelligence-based chat system for realtors.

It enables you to text a unique number on the real estate sign of a property and instantly get a chatbot to give you key answers on the property. The realtor may be with a client or eating dinner with their family. At that very moment this digital assistant with a library of answers is engaging the public in real-time. A potential buyer can text and ask about the "2345 Main Street property" and the chatbot will tell them the square footage, how many rooms, the size of the lot, the height of the ceilings, and then it will ask probing questions in attempt to capture customer data and book a follow-up appointment or virtual or in-person showing.

In the past all these activities were done by the realtor, a salesperson, or a frontline sales assistant, and they are no longer needed. Imagine competing with this realtor! You can handle two inquiries at a time as a realtor with an assistant, but across the street there's a realtor who can handle dozens of concurrent inquiries 24 hours per day, booking meetings and showings while they sleep.

As we fall in love with these tools that can hack and automate our sales process, we're unwittingly being complicit in the complete replacement of the sales profession as we know it. Many aspects of the sales process can be automated and driven by a highly intelligent algorithm. If any of your sales process is repeatable, it can be done by a computer. Cutting and pasting emails, researching company history, entering data from meetings into a CRM are all things that can be done today with very little human input. Our value as sales professionals and sales organizations is not going to come from manually following a process, cutting and pasting messages, setting appointments, or even leaving voicemails. These are sales activities of the past, not the present, and definitely not the future.

Button pushers will be extinct in the world of sales. There are a lot of salespeople right now sitting in cubicles or working remotely from home who are essentially human replacements for a yet-to-be-invented API that connects software programs.

Consider this scenario: A customer who recently inquired on a company website fills out a form. That inquiry is added automatically as a lead in the CRM of a salesperson. The CRM looks for data on that customer buying history and pulls publicly available information about them from the web – automatically populating the database. The CRM then notifies the salesperson of the lead and tells them what template to use based upon a large dataset of successful email follow-ups and then moderately customizes the message. The human salesperson then double checks that the system did it well, and with a push of one button they send the email. Remember Homer Simpson at his desk? Basically that.

When the client opens the email and clicks a specific link, the system tells the salesperson to call them while they are expressing interest. Using another piece of software, it pulls out a script specifically relevant to the product link that was clicked, and the salesperson follows the script or possibly engages in a text-based conversation via LinkedIn, Messenger, or WhatsApp.

Many of the above are left-brain, repeatable activities that don't require the emotional intelligence, creativity, communication skills, objection handling skills, research skills, etc. that sales used to require. It means fewer salespeople are needed.

There's a big chunk of the sales profession that's going to be replaced. Anything left-brained that can be automated, systemized, and made smarter with AI, will be.

This isn't new; in the steel industry, steel factories which used to employ five or six hundred people now employ twenty people who are mostly monitoring the machines and dealing with logistics issues. The machines and systems are doing all the heavy work.

This phenomenon has now moved into the white-collar arena, including sales. People are worried about Uber taking out taxi company jobs, but the reality is that Uber or another company like it, is going to take out drivers altogether. They will do this with vehicles that can drive on their own. They will be arguably safer, more fuel efficient, and easier to maintain as a fleet than a whole bunch of independent representatives who are quickly unionizing in many parts of the world. It's not just sales but multiple industries that are being automated or replaced. Think about how many retail sales jobs Amazon has replaced as well.

There is hope and opportunity. That hope is in the "Right-Brained Sales Revolution." Right-brain selling is creative selling that is based upon innovation and lateral thinking. It's about the people skills and the ability to engage and understand politics, culture, and emotional cues. It's sometimes about breaking the rules and opening up new and unproven markets. This is not something that's going to be automated anytime soon. That face-to-face aspect of selling is something buyers and sellers still love, if it's done well.

If you love selling and you want to be a salesperson five or ten years from now, you've got to think about how you can shift. Shift from being part of the culture of cut-and-paste, following the steps, and pushing buttons to truly becoming indispensable. You become indispensable by fostering and building right-brain sales skills.

If you want to profit and prosper during this sales revolution here are 6 rules you need to observe:

1) IF YOU COMMODIFY YOUR CLIENTS, THEY WILL COMMODIFY YOU.

This is an important insight to embrace. If all of your emails are cut and paste pitches and it's all driven algorithmically by software with the intent of "doing the numbers" you're truly commodifying other human beings (prospects).

The same holds true if you connect to people on LinkedIn and pitch them right away or use a bot that does it for you – pushing out the same generic pitch. If you treat all of your customers like a number, they'll treat you like a number. People know when you have written a personal message and when you have just sent a generic impersonal marketing message out of context.

The quickest way for a salesperson to become dispensable or irrelevant to a customer is for them to have a sense that you're automating and sending generic content or messages. The same holds true if you're sending messages at the wrong time or which are out-of-context.

2) DON'T TRY TO FIT IN, AIM TO BE INDISPENSABLE.

A lot of sales leaders are going to object to this line of thinking, but we believe that you don't just want order takers or yes people in your sales organization. Connect-the-dots salespeople are going to close your average account. The large accounts, new market accounts, and the disruptive opportunities in new industries are going to be driven by your indispensable salespeople, not the people who are good at following the steps taking orders, and cutting and pasting templates. Creative, curious, leaders who have a toolkit of right-brain selling approaches are going to win in new sales environments and turbulent times. These indispensable salespeople are blazing the trail for what will be your new virtual sales playbook, one that may look very different from the one that got you here.

3) IF IT'S PREDICTABLE, DUPLICABLE, AND REPETITIVE IT WILL BE AUTOMATED.

Anything in your sales process that's largely predictable and duplicable will be automated or even driven with artificial intelligence and machine learning. This is not going to happen ten years from now; this is happening now and in the next three to five years we're going to see a massive impact on sales where a whole bunch of work either completely automated or taken over by artificial intelligence. Yes, there will still be salespeople using these tools but one salesperson will be able to do what five or more salespeople do presently. A good chat rep who's not using any type of bot, just typing chat and interacting with customers with the assistance of an answer library can handle up to 7 customers in the same time period a telephone rep can handle one. When you start using artificial intelligence-driven chat solutions (with human back-up) you start to see 1-2 live reps being able to oversee the interaction with 20-30 clients each. The AI handles most of the interaction and the live agent hops in when things go off-script.

Even sales coaching is now being augmented by Artificial Intelligence. To effectively evaluate the sales calls of 20 sales reps a manager or coach would sit through 20+ hours of phone call recordings to see what was happening in the conversations. Tools like Gong.io transcribe all the conversations, look for speech patterns and keywords, and accurately determine which reps are having great profitable conversations and which ones are talking too much. It's all presented in a dashboard to the sales leader and they can quickly dive into key areas… without spending 20 hours evaluating calls. This saves a great deal of time for the sales leader, so they can now focus on the right-brain elevated skills of leadership, coaching, people development, and process iteration. They also have to find something else value added and right-brained to do with the 20 hours a month they saved.

If you ignore AI, big data, automation, and machine learning and just run your sales playbook perfectly you still can't win. If your average rep is outperforming themselves by 40% compared to five years ago BUT your average competitor fully enabled with sales tech is getting the productivity of five reps out of one, there's no comparison. It's like comparing a bulletproof vest and night vision goggles to Tony Stark's Ironman suit. The sales superhero is going to win.

4) PEOPLE SKILLS EAT SALES HACKING SKILLS FOR BREAKFAST.

If everyone is wearing an Ironman suit, then tech is no longer the competitive advantage—it's just your entry fee to the sales conference. There is a time and a place for hacking your sales process; we should be looking for new methods and technology to offload any repetitive sequences and processes (further on in this book we will be talking about building your sales technology stack). Harnessing sales tech tools like Outreach.io and LinkedIn Sales Navigator, you can combine sales intelligence with AI-driven sales sequences that help bring the best leads to you. Eventually, of course, someone has to talk to the prospect *in real life* whether that happens in-person or via a video call. Today it feels like there are more people skilled at creating Tik Tok and Instagram videos than genuine rapport-building. If you have the skills to connect to an individual in a meaningful way, listen well, and build rapport deeply, you have skills that are rarer than the ability to figure out how to hack LinkedIn or Twitter in an automated fashion.

Social selling which involves leveraging social networks and digital channels is more about people skills than understanding all of the little hacks and tricks on each network. One of the big failures for most in social selling is the over-automation of content postings and conversations.

Shane shares: "I started in the social media space back in 2002 with blogging and podcasting in 2004. Steve Jagger and I wrote the book "Sociable!" in 2009. It was one the very first books on social media for sales professionals and entrepreneurs. The whole premise of the book was to use the internet to get off of the internet. What we meant by that was start the relationship digitally but realize that the ROI is most likely going to be realized when we finally meet in-person or have an in-depth video conference."

We need to find ways to humanize our sales process even while leveraging technology to do it better.

5) STOP DOING THE WRONG THINGS BETTER.

Minto Roy, CEO of Social Print paper said, "the problem with most sales organizations is they're trying to do the wrong thing better."

Most of your competitors are trying to squeeze the uniqueness out of their sales team, most are applying a "one size fits all" sales process to people and companies they are focused on. To increase revenues, they try to find ways to double the number of prospect interactions instead of improving effectiveness. The problem is, many of their prospects and clients have their own unique buying process and don't fit into a typical sales funnel. The wrong thing is to treat your customers like a number by failing to invest time evaluating the customer and customize the message and engagement. Stop trying to scale the wrong thing better than your competitors. Instead, find ways to personalize, add depth, and engage with the right context.

Many organizations are happy if they convert 3-5% of their prospects. Instead of improving the conversion rate through better engagement and context, most will opt to just spend more time, money, and energy on a larger number of prospects. This is a wasteful approach. We are offending or repelling 95% of the people we talk to looking for the easy converts using a generic process. This is the opposite of playing the long game in sales.

The question you need to ask is "How do I employ my creativity and communications skills to be indispensable to my clients, my employer, and my industry – and what technologies can help me do this?"

6) RELATIONSHIPS SCALE, FOLLOWERS DON'T.

The new arms race in sales and marketing is reach and content production. Everyone is in a race to generate a ton of leads and to find new and interesting ways to grow their LinkedIn connection numbers. They believe the more connections or followers we have, the more influence or leads we have. This is only partially true. It's not about having 30,000 connections; it's about having 30 raving fans who love the work you've done for them or their business. Each of them with 10,000 connections can share your content, the value you bring to the table, and get you in front of their audiences and communities. That's how social truly scales: you do good work, develop deeper relationships, and those people talk about you.

7) THE LEFT-BRAIN QUALIFIES THE BUYER AND THE RIGHT-BRAIN QUALIFIES THE SELLER.

In a customer discovery call or needs analysis much of the qualification conversation is a left-brained activity. It doesn't add value, it simply measures the value of the client opportunity. It answers the question: "Is this prospect qualified to buy from us and what do we have that they need?" The right-brain on the other hand qualifies the seller. By being creative, empathetic, socially intelligent, and willing to challenge the customers thinking we position ourselves as a resource and trusted advisor. We do this by offering insights based upon our deep understanding of the customer, our solutions, and the personalized way we can help them.

8) YOU CANNOT BE LEAPFROGGED BY PEOPLE IF YOU'RE AHEAD OF THEM BY 10,000 HOURS.

It's easy to learn new technologies. You can hack things together, build a better CRM, or buy a better automated prospecting system than a competitor. You can also hire someone to build you a solid sales tech stack and process map. Your competitor can easily catch up or even leapfrog your technological advantage by spending more money or finding a better AI-based selling too. You can't, however, pay someone else to make you better (overnight) at rapport building, negotiating, or being creative and innovative. It takes time, practice, feedback, and ongoing effort to improve our "Social Intelligence."

Investing in our salespeople's SI (Social Intelligence) is key; screening for it during the interview process is vital. This quote from Daniel Goleman author of Social Intelligence sums it up well, "If your emotional abilities aren't in hand, if you don't have self-awareness, if you are not able to manage your distressing emotions, if you can't have empathy and have effective relationships, then no matter how smart you are, you are not going to get very far."

If you've been working for five years straight, very focused on developing your person to person selling skills, emotional intelligence, negotiation skills, listening abilities, etc. a new person on the block can't leapfrog you and be just as good as you overnight. You can't buy social intelligence and soft skills. The art of selling, persuasion, social intelligence, and other right-brained sales skills keep you ahead and make you indispensable. A competitor may utilize CRM better or find a new way to hack a sales prospecting process, but none of that matters when you get in that boardroom or Zoom meeting. Your 10,000 more hours invested in the soft skills of selling are what will help you close that deal.

Here is an expansive, but not all-inclusive, list of the right-brained sales skills and strengths that will give you the edge. As a sales leader reading this list, think about your sales team and how many of them possess these traits. If you're in sales, read this list, make a note of which of these you possess, which ones you would like to acquire, and which ones you need to refine or upskill.

Below are 27 right-brained sales skills or areas of talents; underneath that there's a quick grading template where you can assess your own level of competency in right-brain sales skills or use it as a quick template to review the people on your team or potential hires for their capacity to be right-brained sales pros.

27 RIGHT-BRAINED SALES SKILLS AND TALENTS

1. **Rapport Building**: The ability to establish rapport is vital. It is the foundation of trust building; without it, most relationships in business or our personal lives will not get a chance to start.

2. **Listening**: Great salespeople listen more than they talk. Through listening they can deepen understanding, identify buying motives, and expand customer trust and engagement.

3. **Social Intelligence (Sales SI)**: Daniel Goleman in his seminal book describes "Social Intelligence" as "social awareness, what we sense about others, and social facility, what we then do with that awareness." It's not just about being aware of ourselves and others; it's about putting that awareness into action to produce a sales result.

4. **Presentation Skills**: Getting in front of an audience in a boardroom, conference, or Zoom meeting and engaging and persuading an audience is a coveted talent. Its unique and humanized elements are something that will always be needed.

5. **Objection Handling Skills**: Objection handling is problem solving. Client solutions and even product innovations are born out of objections. Some might even argue that if there were no objections there would be no need for salespeople: we would all be in customer service.

6. **Negotiations**: One of the highest paid skills in business. Negotiations is about leaving the other person feeling like they have won, while still closing a profitable deal. It's one-part chess and one-part human psychology.

7. **Hobnobbing**: A term rarely used this day but still an important skill. It's the ability to network and socialize our way into a more affluent or powerful sphere of influence. It's about social rules, rapport, strategy, and community.

8. **Online social interaction and engagement**: Having genuine or atypical online conversations and interactions get us noticed. They help us connect with prospects and deepen client relationships. A bot might be helpful when shopping online but they're not useful for the truly "social" aspect of social media and social networks. It's essentially about talking to our customers on the internet while adding value in the context of the relationship.

9. **Innovating**: This is about seeing unmet needs and developing new solutions through inspiration, creativity, and instinct. It's not about following a map: it's about creating a new one.

10. **Problem Solving**: This skill is about looking at a specific situation or challenge that is new for the client and collaboratively developing a solution or new direction.

11. **Detecting Lies**: Being able to spot a lie, a half-truth, or just seeing that someone is holding back is an important sales and sales leadership trait. This is done through being in tune with body language, cultures, speech patterns, and other varied cues.

12. **Reading and Adjusting for Style**: Reading personality styles can help us identify how people buy. It's then about shifting our communication style and sales process to be aligned with them.

13. **Contextualizing Offers and Solutions**: Personalizing and customizing solutions can be done in an almost infinite number of ways. Every customer is a VIP (Very Individual Person) and customization helps them buy into what we are offering.

14. **Breaking the Rules**: Sometimes to win you need to break the rules or the sales process. Many deals have been won because a salesperson skipped steps 3-6 in a 7-step sales process because that's what felt right at the moment.

15. **Humor**: This probably should have been #1. It's a human trait that when applied correctly has opened a lot of doors and won many hearts. It's an art, and humor is ever evolving with our society.

16. **Giving**: Helping others, genuinely contributing to community, and also desiring to see our clients succeed is something that people can feel. Knowing that someone truly cares about us can motivate us to do business with them. Seeing the need and filling it in the right way is key.

17. **Managing Complex Business Relationships (Selling to multiple stakeholders)**: As deals get bigger so do the politics and number of people involved. This type of selling is about generating consensus and support from a diverse group of people who have common and competing goals. Complex sales are about "buy-in" from multiple people with different personalities and needs.

18. **Phone Skills**: One-to-one phone skills are another important soft skill. A phone call will continue to be a very human, high touch aspect of communications. It's especially important for the more camera-shy customers who don't love Zoom or Skype video calls.

19. **Dealing with Upset Customers**: As a customer, when you are irate you don't want to talk to a robot. De-fusing and redirecting customer frustration into a positive outcome are vital.

20. **Motivating Team Members**: This skill, talent, and mindset comes from having the heart of a leader and coach. These salespeople might be focused on closing deals and hitting quotas, but they also uplift and mentor their team members as well.

21. **Going Off Script**: Living in the moment and taking actions based upon good sales instincts and principles is an important skill when we are in uncharted territory. It especially applies to situations where your sales process isn't serving the customer. It's about carving out a new approach, in the moment.

22. **Needs Analysis Selling / Discovery Selling**: Bill Gibson called this 70/30 selling. It's a process where you interview the customer, listen more than you talk, and establish yourself as a trusted advisor. This includes the ability to unearth deep motivations and hidden objections.

23. **Authentic Relationship Development (NOT ABM or lead nurturing)**: Simply put, this is about making friends and developing long lasting relationships. It's a life skill and a sales skill. Many relationships will far outlast the products we sell or the organizations we work for.

24. **Content creation**: Social selling and communicating on social channels is another right-brained skill. Creative content creation is part of that skills set.

25. **Networking in Real Life**: Meeting people in person at events, conferences, and in the community will never go out of style.

26. **Curious Prospecting (Motivated lateral thinking)**: Being curious is about finding new places to network, new alliances, and innovative ways to connect with hard to reach prospects.

27. **Personal Branding and Reputation Building**: People buy from people. Our personal reputation, credibility, and track record are important currencies in a marketplace where people are unsure about who and what to believe.

RIGHT-BRAIN SALES COMPETENCY ASSESSMENT

Instructions:

For each statement, place an "X" to rate your team or team member on a scale of 1-5 where:

1 = Strongly disagree 2 = Disagree 3 = Neutral 4 = Agree 5 = Strongly agree in relation to each trait listed below. Once again this can be used for recruiting or assessing existing team members or organizing a dream team for a strategic project or new market entry.

Right-Brained Sales Skills	1	2	3	4	5
Rapport Building					
Listening					
Social Intelligence (Sales SI)					
Presentation Skills					
Objection Handling Skills					
Negotiations					
Hobnobbing					
Online social interaction and engagement					
Innovating					
Problem Solving					
Detecting Lies					
Reading and Adjusting for Style					
Contextualizing Offers and Solutions					
Breaking the Rules					
Humor					
Giving					
Managing Complex Business Relationships					
Phone Skills					
Dealing with Upset Customers					
Motivating Team Members					
Going Off Script					
Needs Analysis Selling / Discovery Selling					
Authentic Relationship Development					
Content creation					
Networking in Real Life					
Curious Prospecting (Motivated lateral thinking)					
Personal Branding and Reputation Building					
Totals:					

Sales leaders and executives reading this might be asking, "Why would I want a bunch of unruly right-brained salespeople on my team?" It's true that leading creative and sometimes non-compliant types is challenging. You can't just give them marching orders and watch them comply. Here's a few reasons why it might be worth it:

1) They are proactive, not reactive button pushers. During crisis or upheaval, they don't wait around to be told what to do. They're going to act proactively to generate the sales results they want. These people don't typically wait around for marketing to hand them leads or to develop new markets and opportunities. You don't have to spoon-feed them. They stay up at night thinking about how they can get better at selling. They're the ones sitting in the front row when you hold a training event and even though they have the most experience they're taking notes looking for the next little piece that's going to give them an edge.

2) They are action, not entitlement, focused. They have few excuses. If they experience a setback or miss a quota, they're not going to blame marketing or the competition. They will likely have a suggested solution to any challenge or problem. This comes from their creative and curious nature.

3) They are adaptable. Flexibility is a key characteristic of the right-brained salesperson. That combined with curiosity makes them great lifelong learners. Whether it's a new target market or learning the latest technology they will lean into the change not resist it.

4) They improve products and processes. As client-centric innovators they are always looking for new ways to serve clients and the additional revenues that come with that. They're the first to point out how a process could be improved or what types of offerings your clients are looking for now and in the future. They think like a business owner or intrapreneur.

5) They lead customers versus take orders. Using engaging needs assessment processes and deep insights the right-brained salesperson creatively leads the customer through the buyer's journey. Rarely will they put themselves in a situation where they sell a product or service without making sure it's the most relevant solution for the customer.

6) They close more business. Linear thinking order takers rarely maximize selling opportunities. They're happy following the process and wait to be told what their customer wants. You need collaborative people skills and a solution creation mindset to close bigger deals.

7) They grow accounts through focused relationship and credibility building. They apply their communications, rapport, and collaborative skill sets to add value and deepen relationships. They realize that it's not just about likability, it's about business credibility.

8) They use technology but are driven by principles. Your right-brained sales leader will not shy away from learning and applying new technology. It's in their nature to find easier ways to do things. With that said, they creatively apply tech to help them in their sales process – they won't let tech lead or limit their processes.

9) They come with a network and credibility (from their past successes). Because they come with a toolkit of right-brained sales skills most will have a vast network of connections. They will come to work on the first day and bring their network and their credibility with them.

As a sales leader don't be afraid of recruiting these dynamic sales innovators. Instead, work on developing your abilities as a right-brained sales leader. You're not trying to manage them; you're going to lead them. The skills set, attitudes, and competencies for leaders we talked about in previous chapters are your toolkit to lead this next generation of sales pros.

CHAPTER 7

BEING A BRAND LEADER IN A FRAGMENTED VIRTUAL MARKETPLACE

Today one of the biggest challenges for organizations, individual marketers, and sales professionals is to get noticed. Many of us recently have had to deal with the reality that we no longer can rely on in person meetings, customers walking through our door, and serendipitous opportunities to connect through community events, socializing, or industry conferences. Face to face in-person networking, sales, and marketing was one of the things that we excelled at.

For some of us there has been a gradual shifting to the virtual space over the last decade or longer. For most of us though 2020 was a year where we went from virtual and digital marketing being a contributor to our marketing and sales success to being a primary channel and in many cases our only channel to connect to potential existing clients and service them.

As authors and speakers in 2019 about 20% of our income came from online programs, webinars, and digital products. In 2020 less than 15% of our revenues have been offline or generated from physical products or in-person training. That's a huge shift. A senior executive at Purolator Courier which is the largest Courier company in Canada recently shared with us some very similar statistics about Purolator. In 2018 and 2019 approximately 20% of their packages shipped were delivered to the home of the consumer by their clients, the other 80% of shipments were business to business. In 2020 80% of Purolator shipments were direct from corporations to consumers' homes. These are two examples of rapid shifts in the marketplace driven by a boom in virtual service delivery and ecommerce platforms. This incredible change is unlikely to reverse anytime soon. We are now in a very virtual, digital, and ecommerce driven sales environment. To compete we need to understand how to leverage these networks to reach, engage, and do business with our ideal clients.

The digital tools and platforms that many organizations have used recently to pivot online and become virtually competitive enterprises, are generally not new platforms.

113

These platforms, ecommerce tools, and social networking sites have been around for many years and are quite powerful if you know how to use them. The great thing about these tools is they are very accessible and many are free or nearly free, those that are paid tools are bargains once you know how to use them as well. That's the good news - the bad news is everyone else has access to these tools. It's getting busy online and the platforms are getting more and more crowded. The number of platforms and channels are growing daily, with high competition. There is almost limitless content being created and shared and limitless products and services to be discovered. Clients and customers have almost endless choices and options at the click of a button, their attention is fragmented across multiple channels, and our competitors are on those channels as well.

The key is to rise above the noise, our goal is to develop a unique signal or beacon that attracts and engages our ideal customer and client segments. This strategy to rise above requires three key components or areas of focus as a brand. These components are:

Hyper segmentation: The ability to measurably identify who your true ideal clients are and understand how you can uniquely and competitively meet their needs, solve their problems, and help them reach their goals.

Thought Leadership: Being a thought leader is about building a community driven brand, that is not just seen as a product peddler but a trusted resource and authority in your chosen market segments.

Leveraging the New Sales Funnel with Social Selling: The new sales funnel is completely, community, conversation, and content driven. Understanding this new virtual sales process will help you gain trust, credibility, and consent to market and sell to your ideal clients.

YOU CAN'T BOIL THE OCEAN — GET FOCUSED ON YOUR NANOTRIBES

We need to be able to answer three very important questions before we even consider launching an online presence. These questions are:

1) **Who is your ideal customer?** Can you quantify this down almost at a cellular level?

2) **Who are your competitors?** Do you understand your direct and indirect competitors in each of the channels and platforms you choose to sell and market in?

3) **Is your business product or service a nice to have or is it a pill?** Pills solve pains. Do you truly understand your customers' pains, challenges, and goals, and how your solution is going to competitively and uniquely help them reach their goal or solve a problem?

The fantastic opportunity that social networks and platforms offer is that you can reach almost any conceivable market, and test and launch almost any idea, product or service, reaching literally any corner of the world you want to. You can't boil the ocean; you have to strategically and consciously choose what small corner of this massive sea of opportunity that you're going to focus on.

Because there's so many people online, and there's so much content you have to dig deep and define content that's relevant to your business or personal life. This is the challenge that many of our customers and clients are facing, they're trying to articulate what they need and then find it. If you've ever searched for anything on the Internet, you'll know that good research or procurement requires the ability to filter out everything that's not 100% relevant to your needs. Your clients and customers are doing this and what this means to you is that you need to make sure that your offerings, your messaging, and even your social networking are hyper-focused in a way to make sure that they can find you, and that your messaging and communications get noticed. It's advisable that you start with understanding your ideal client groups and then work your strategy backward from there. It's not enough to be just generic in your targeting nor have a general idea of who your ideal customers are going to be.

When building your online marketing, sales, and brand strategy it's easy to just think in terms of general niches but even Coca-Cola with $100 million marketing budgets cannot afford to market to the entire planet or be too general. They understand their Nanotribes and create messaging and engagement specific to their needs, culture, region, and values. We need to drill down to our Nanotribes. These are small subsets of people or companies that make up a larger niche. Most successful digital brands will have a core brand strategy but under its umbrella will be 4-5 Nanotribe strategies with slightly different offerings, messaging, and engagement methods. We have all heard of the Pareto Principle or 80/20 rule, where 80% of your profit is going to come from 20% of your clients. Today it's more like 90/10, and if we don't find a way to focus and be truly relevant to that 10%, we may not be in business long.

For a mid-sized IT company in a city like Seattle there are almost endless opportunities to sell, manage services, and technology solutions. If one were to ask that IT business owner who their ideal client is, they may say something like mid to large size companies in the Seattle area. If you were trying to bring this person business or develop a marketing strategy it's likely that you would bring them more bad leads than good leads. One of the things that keeps small businesses small is the many hours and resources it takes to service customers that aren't ideal.

We want to focus our efforts so that we target companies where we have an unfair advantage or unique value proposition for them. It's important to understand who we would be most desirable to. Picking a niche, specializing in it, and then breaking it down into Nanotribes so we can develop unique sound bites and solutions for those subgroups enables us to be a big fish in the ponds of our choosing. Instead of having generic targeting criteria such as I'm targeting companies in the Seattle area (there are 97,000 of them) this owner could drill down further to define who these Nanotribes are and how their business can uniquely serve them. Here's an example of a micro niche or Nanotribe for an IT company:

- Enterprises with 60 or more employees
- Those who are growing or are in a high growth segment
- In the medical services industry
- With four or more locations
- Those who are located within 15 miles of one of our service offices

- Are presently looking to undergo a full digital transformation
- Those who handles sensitive client data that needs to be protected

Now with their marketing and sales efforts this IT company doesn't have to communicate what they do to 97,000 potential customers many of whom are not profitable. They won't be dealing with companies with needs beyond the capabilities of the firm. There are probably 200 companies of that 97,000 which would be in the Nanotribe described above. If they had 4-5 well designed segments as above, they would be able to focus their efforts and develop their expertise in a meaningful way and build a dominant position in those Nanotribes.

By defining your segments this forensically you can now create marketing content and sales outreach strategies that talk specifically to this market. It's possible to build an expertise around this market segment that makes you the #1 solution provider. Most businesses don't need 97,000 customers, they need a handful of profitable and loyal ones. Those profitable clients are distracted and overwhelmed, so by focusing on them and sharpening your message and expertise, you are a signal that rises above the noise.

Following is a template to help you define your Nanotribes, it will help you define one, but we suggest you take the time to define 4-5 that you will be targeting and engaging online. First develop 4-5 criteria that will define your Nanotribe, then identify their core needs and goals and the solutions you can provide to help them. Finally list your key competitors in that segment and how you intend to compete or position yourself.

DEFINE YOUR NANOTRIBES:

Nanotribe:	
Criteria 1	
Criteria 2	
Criteria 3	
Criteria 4	
Criteria 5	
Notes:	
Needs, goals and characteristics of this Nanotribe:		
Need, Goal, or Challenge?	How can we help?	What are the expected results?

Who are my competitors in this segment and how will I compete?		
Competitor	Their strengths and weaknesses?	How will we compete?

Once you have defined your Nanotribe and understand their core needs, values, and goals we are now ready to begin building our brand and engaging them online.

BUILDING A BRAND IN A FRAGMENTED MARKETPLACE

In today's virtual sales environment, our brand is much less about big media buys, logos, catchy jingles, and even viral videos. Those are all traditional methods of evaluating a brand. A brand was something that we polished refined, then through big media storytelling and a lot of money spent on advertising and collateral, we bombarded the marketplace with that brand message, tone, and brand promise. After enough frequency of contact and exposure to it began to sink into the psyche of our customer in the marketplace. This type of bombardment required attention, and often came from a small number of channels, such as print radio and even online driven advertising.

Today a truly strong brand does require financial investment and still benefits from traditional advertising whether that's offline or offline. With that said the brands that are truly morphing into market leaders or reinventing themselves to maintain their relevance are all realizing that investing in thought leadership is vital.

Your client today has an extremely fragmented attention span. It's not about shopping online or offline when we think about fragmentation, you will find that even in ecommerce regardless of someone's demographic- they all shop in a fragmented fashion. They'll spend some time on Amazon, then hop onto an traditional retailers ecommerce site, then scroll through Instagram, and all of a sudden find themselves with one click in a micro ecommerce site where they can purchase directly through Instagram. Then they find themselves on a deals app looking for the latest discounts that will drop ship to them from anywhere in the world.

This is the fragmented attention of today's consumer, they're spending their dollars across multiple platforms, and their attention resides on multiple social networks over short periods of time. They get their news from Twitter, their fashion inspiration from Instagram, and spend hours conversing on LinkedIn, Facebook, and within WhatsApp messenger. This is why blockbuster mentality marketing efforts don't work. This antiquated method is about buying out a channel and then hammering the consumer over and over again, doesn't work anymore because they're not sticking around that long.

People are overwhelmed by the sheer volume of communications content and messages coming at them every hour, so if you come on strong from an Internet perspective, they tend to tune you out, mute you, or unfollow you. Investing in being in only one channel almost guarantees that we're going to miss out on the attention of our marketplace 9 out of 10 times. There are demographics that live on one or two channels or are unique to that channel. Today we are in what would be called an omnichannel everything environment; people don't just use one channel to social network or connect with their peers, to shop or research their purchases or potential purchases, nor for communications sharing information or connecting with communities.

Branding today is not about dominating one social channel like Facebook, or about creating viral videos that make you more memorable than your competitor. Today your brand is the most valuable thing you have, more than your marketing strategies or your sales tactics. With that said your brand is something that is a bit more nebulous than it was in the past, borrowing a quote from Bestselling author and Father of Guerrilla Marketing Jay Conrad Levinson, "*your brand is what your customer says it is.*" Jay said this many years ago but today it's truer than ever. Customer reviews, online comments on Twitter, recommendations people are making to their friends, and unsolicited product testimonials or positive shout-outs from happy clients are all now part of your brand. Not only are they part of your brand they are actually the leading drivers of your brand.

Your brand is now a living and dynamically changing sentiment indicator which represents your overall community experience with your organization on all platforms, social networks, and relevant ecommerce channels. If your brand is what your customer says it is - it's important to note that what your customer says it is has everything to do with what their individual experiences are with your brand. We would take it a step further and say that today your brand isn't just what your customer says it is, your brand is with the community says it is, so it's about the community experience of your brand long before and after they make the purchase, most of the brand experience will not be during the transaction or even use of your product or service.

Today most of our customers or clients will make the majority of their buying decision, including researching our brand, engaging our team, and looking for direction and advice on that purchase, virtually. Online thought leadership is one of the key elements of a strong brand and if established well can help us find new clients, grow existing client relationships, drive referrals, and retain business. This online brand greatly contributes to employee attraction and retention. We have spent a fair bit of time talking about the need for this new dynamic method of branding but let's now spend a little bit of time finding what thought leadership truly is and some of the action steps you're going to take as an organization to become a thought leader in your chosen markets.

BRANDS AS THOUGHT LEADERS AND YOUR PEOPLE AS ONLINE BRANDS

Thought leadership is a buzzword that has almost saturated the marketplace especially for those of us in any marketing and sales space. It's important for us to define what establishing your brand as a thought leader means in the context of being competitive in the virtual economy.

When we say that your brand needs to position itself as a thought leader, what we are saying is that you need to leverage three key elements of the modern brand that will build massive trust, relevancy, and a sense of magnetism that actually retains your existing clients, encourages them to talk about your brand, and draws new clients and customers to your brand community. We will get to those three elements in a few pages.

A "Thought Leader" is an expert who through their strong leadership and communications skills has established a high level of credibility, trust, and influence in a specific community related to their area of expertise. This area of expertise could be in making the world's best tasting non-alcoholic craft beer, accounting software, or even being a thought leader in the area of engaging and entertaining online events.

Thought leadership is also proven to drive ROI in a B2B marketing and sales context. In the Edelman Study on "2019 B2B Thought Leadership Impact Study" they uncovered some compelling results from their analysis of over 1200 organizations. Here is a selection of their findings:

- 47% of C-suite executives shared their contact information after viewing a piece of thought leadership content.
- 45% invited an organization to bid on a project after not previously considering them.
- 58% of decision makers reported that thought leadership directly led them to award business to an organization.
- 61% of C-suite executives are more willing to pay a premium to work with an organization that has articulated a clear vision versus one that doesn't invest in thought leadership.
- 58% of senior decision makers spend 1 or more hour reading thought leadership content weekly. 28% spend 4+ hours a week.

Content not cold-calls may be your best bet to virtually access coveted senior business decision makers.

What you're selling and passionate about as an organization is what you can establish yourself as a thought leader in. Your thought leadership doesn't have to be broadly appealing; it just has to reach out and grab your target markets attention. You don't have to be a motivational speaker or a Pulitzer Prize winner to be a thought leader, you just have to be a person or corporation with

> **Content not cold-calls may be your best bet to virtually access coveted senior business decision makers.**

unique expertise who is able to leverage that expertise through online branding to become a household name in your niche and respective Nanotribes. As a result, people seek you out for help, guidance, and leadership in your area of expertise. What's important to note is that your individual team members' level of Thought Leadership is inseparable from your brand's thought leadership and identity.

Customer or client experience directly impacts individual sentiment about your brand. Something as simple as what your accountant shares on Instagram about a day in the life of an accountant in your place of business has an impact on your brand and either contributes or detracts from your thought leadership in the marketplace. Let's take a look at the elements of establishing yourself as an online thought leader, and how you can equip your people to contribute to and accelerate your positioning in the marketplace as a thought leader above your competitors.

Thought leaders from the context of how we define them must do three things well:

1) **Thought Leaders create and curate relevant content** on an ongoing basis that is posted and shared through multiple channels, those channels of course depend upon where your existing and future clients and customers are or will be putting their attention.

2) **Great thought leaders have relevant engaging conversations** with their customers, clients, and community at large. They call it social media not broadcast media for a reason, broadcast media is about pushing messages out to the marketplace essentially yelling at our customer hopefully louder than our competitors do. Social media is a two-way communication medium. Great thought leadership-oriented brands know that part of establishing that strong brand and community experience is going to happen through all of the conversations we have within multiple communications channels and platforms.

3) **Thought leaders build community**. Community building from a brand perspective is essentially doing things that are bigger than your brand. What that means is that ideally your brand is either morphed into a movement or champions major movements or initiatives in the marketplace. Community building is about the continual and systematic expansion of the number of people in your community and our reach. It goes without saying that it is obviously not just about numbers but the quality of individuals and organizations that we would consider part of our community.

THE FOLLOWING MODEL OUTLINES THREE THINGS GREAT THOUGHT LEADERS DO VERY WELL:

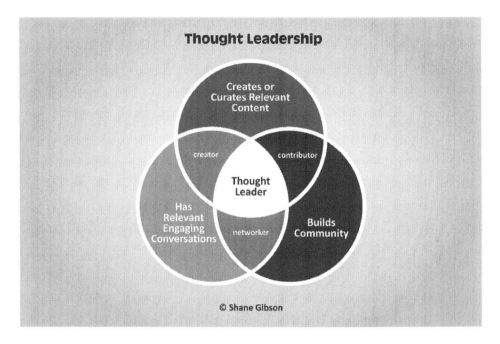

Let's dive into each of these competencies and core activities a bit deeper:

GREAT THOUGHT LEADERS CREATE AND CURATE CONTENT:

Your content must speak specifically to solving key problems, meeting core goals, solving pains, and/or emotionally evoking the passion of your core target markets. This will include content created by your marketing team, vendors and suppliers, strategic alliances, and industry experts. To rise above the online noise, the content you author or curate must resonate specifically with your core Nanotribe category prospects and centers of influence in your chosen markets. The more general your content the more likely it will never be noticed or valued.

Content can be a blog post, LinkedIn article, a Facebook update, Instagram video, or even a whitepaper on a certain aspect of investing. It doesn't always have to be your content, sharing great insights from another person or brand within your network verifies that you're not just there to promote your self-serving content, you're there to help and add value. What we do know from research done by Edelman is that "57% of decision makers said their preferred format for thought leadership is "snackable" media that can be digested in a few minutes." "Popcorn content" as Nick Usborne refers to it, is easier to produce than deep content or elaborate productions.

Some of the types of content you can create could include:

1) Blog posts, videos, or even white papers that help answer common and frequently asked questions about your business industry or products and services. This could be presented as a series of Instagram videos, stories, or even multiple images posted as a sequence. Depending on your demographic you could creatively answer your FAQ's in short Tik Tok videos and then share those to other channels that have similar format videos.

2) Day in the life of posts: these are behind the scenes pictures, videos, short LinkedIn posts, or a myriad of other updates that show snapshots of daily activities behind the scenes in your business.

3) Whitepapers and research: this type of content proves to be valuable when targeting business to business decision makers. Brief summaries and small pieces of content based upon deeper work are popular.

4) Voice of customer: this could be a customer testimonial, an explainer video showing how a customer has used or implemented your product or service, or even just a screen captured tweet from a happy customer or stakeholder.

5) Expert interviews: interviewing experts via LinkedIn live, a Zoom meeting, or even publishing an interview with an expert from an offline event online are popular types of content depending upon your market vertical. These bigger interviews then can broken-down into dozens of sound bite and quotes that can be shared in various formats over time.

6) Podcasts: creating your own corporate podcast that could be DIY focused or provide business intelligence and even entertainment can be an effective way to engage your target audience. Some organizations have done very well just getting some of their senior executives on popular podcasts and then re-purposing those interviews as micro content, white papers, or eBooks.

7) How To's and list posts: if you own a CRM software company a post on top ten ways to improve your sales prospecting or how to reach important corporate decision makers is an engaging type of content that you will find get shared and read a lot. Even more importantly is some of the most effective how-to or list posts often have nothing to do with your business but are of great value to your target market. Someone like Ford Motor Company could put out a video safety series on preparing for and driving in the winter, mentioning very little about their product specifically but providing great value and positive association or experience with their brand as a result.

8) Interactive tools like quizzes, polls, or self-assessments: an IT company who is marketing their services could provide a free online assessment on cybersecurity, or data security and provide the customer a score and a series of action steps that they could take to make their business more secure. These types of interactive assessments polls and quizzes are entertaining but also allow people to interact with your brand and get customized value out of that interaction. Think about ways that you could add these to your social channels and websites.

Without turning this whole chapter into a chapter on content marketing we want to just give you a few examples of the types of content that you could be and should be creating for your organization regularly. One of the things we said earlier is that if you're not visible on social networks or through search to potential customers, you don't exist. By creating, curating, and sharing value-added content that helps your customer avoid pain, some problem, reach a goal, or learn something new, we have the opportunity to create positive community experience around our brand.

Unfortunately, we can't create one or two pieces of great content a month and then sit back and watch the community grow. With the amount of noise on social channels and various platforms your content strategy has to be frequent, constantly evolving, and present across the many channels that our target clients, stakeholders, and existing customers divide their attention.

Content Marketing Tip: Create and curate content with your client in mind. Get inside their head and heart and deeply reflect on what would truly add value and help them in a unique way. Better content will always under-perform compared to unique content.

> **Content Marketing Tip:** Create and curate content with your client in mind. Get inside their head and heart and deeply reflect on what would truly add value and help them in a unique way. Better content will always under-perform compared to unique content.

THE POWER OF PERSONAL THOUGHT LEADERSHIP

One of the things that will slow down the true potential of your organization as a thought leader in your area of expertise and chosen markets is the need to control or dampen the voice of your individual employees, customers, and community members. There's been much research done on the influence of individual employees over that of corporate brands. The consensus based upon research (plus anecdotal feedback from the marketplace) is that most people put more merit in what an individual employee may say to them than the official brand messaging from that corporation. People buy from people, whether it's on a retail store floor, a tradeshow, or in a LinkedIn messenger conversation.

Earlier in the book we shared statistics and insights on the importance of building brand advocacy online by encouraging your employees to share a day in the life at work, share their expertise within your industry, and of course official corporate content like white papers, or a video outlining a customer success story. In most cases you'll find that an employee's social networks only slightly overlap with that of the official corporate brand or other employees in that organization. What that means is that you can expand the reach of your brand and the community's experience of it by harnessing the power of your crowd (staff).

Imagine if your official LinkedIn account for your Corporation had 5000 followers, and then let's for arguments sake say that you had 10 sales pros on your team that each had 2000 LinkedIn connections. Most research points to the fact that about 20% of any one of your employees' personal connections may be following your brand as well on various social channels. What that means is that only 400 of each of your sales teams 2000 LinkedIn connections are actually following your official brand updates. Each sales professional can literally introduce your brand and share your content and insights with an additional 1600 people, that's collectively an additional 16,000 people in reach through your sales team. Of course, it doesn't just end at your sales team, your accounting team could enthusiastically share some of your brand content, so could frontline customer service people, middle management, and even some of your vendors and partners. The social reach of the individuals within your organization in most cases can be 5, 10, or even 20 times larger than your official corporate accounts. As noted earlier, this type of sharing must be natural, and in context with what your individual employees and stakeholders feel is relevant to their audience and their comfort zone. Not all employees will share all content all the time, but if you put a good enough content development program together (ideally collaboratively with your team), they will want to share and contribute to that content ecosystem.

"Brand messages are re-shared 24 X more and reach 561% further when posted and shared by employees."
– POSTBEYOND.COM "EMPLOYEE ADVOCACY GUIDE"

One of the more powerful ways to create long term inbound sales funnels is to enable and equip those members of your team in sales, marketing, and other customer facing positions to individually establish themselves as thought leaders. Through curating and even creating unique content, sales team members can help themselves move from being an order taker or salesperson to being seen as a resource and an expert. With a little guidance and a good social media policy your sales team members can create content from their perspective - they can begin to help tell a brand story about your organization from the ground level.

Being positioned as a Thought Leader can help a salesperson "sit down" toe-to-toe (or screen-to-screen) with a senior executive and be appreciated as someone who is knowledgeable in the industry and can provide much needed guidance. This occurs because that decision maker has been able to see and consume that sales team members individual unique content and curated content on various social networks.

A lot of organizations have fallen in love with the concept of influencer marketing which we will mention and go into a little bit later on in this chapter. The challenge with a lot of influencers is that only a small percentage of their audience may be your target audience, plus depending upon what you're selling or marketing, they may only have a limited understanding or expertise of your offering and can't intelligently field questions or give advice to people who want to learn more.

One of the challenges of influencer marketing is they may be talking about your product but it's still difficult to segue one of their community members' interests expressed in a conversation to getting them into your sales funnel or even capturing their personal information. Establishing your own employees as thought leaders in your specific area of expertise is actually a way to build an influencer in house - in many cases it will be a group of influencers. They understand your products, services, and client personas at a much greater depth than a generic influencer. We're not bashing influencers. We highly suggest that you find ways to leverage them; why not build your own internal team of influencers who are loyal and on-brand? By encouraging numerous staff to be influencers it is a risk mitigation strategy. If you have only one or two and they leave you're vulnerable.

As a CEO or senior leader, it's vital that you're walking the talk and producing and sharing content as well. Companies with senior leaders active on social media build more trust with customers than those that don't. This also extends to their own team as it provides a direct channel for feedback and engagement and is essentially a digital open-door policy.

Here are some key stats on why C-level executives need to get involved in social media:

- 65% of US employees say it's important for CEOs to actively communicate about their companies online, particularly during times of crisis. – BusinessInsider.com
- 60% of employees say they would check an executive's social media before joining a company. – BusinessInsider.com.
- "75% of consumers say a CEO's presence on social makes a brand more trustworthy" – Hootsuite Study "The Social Executive"
- "Companies with leaders active on social media are 23% more positively perceived than companies with inactive leaders." – Hootsuite Study "The Social Executive"

GREAT THOUGHT LEADERS HAVE GREAT CONVERSATIONS.

Content is not enough. Conversation builds and deepens relationships and fosters dialogue with your target market. Conversation creates more content and exposure. A process of eliciting feedback and generating conversation needs to be implemented as a daily discipline on major social media channels. This is an activity for your marketing team, and for individual staff who've taken the leap into the world of social networks and made the decision to establish themselves as thought leaders. For your sales team, savvy social sellers know they have to be proactive, focused, and strategic about who they engage in dialogue and do it every day on the key social platforms they use. A recent in-depth study by LinkedIn showed that active social sellers far outperform their peers that don't:

WAYS SALES TEAM MEMBERS COULD START CONVERSATIONS USING SOCIAL MEDIA:

Connect with your clients and prospects on LinkedIn and monitor their updates. When the client or prospect posts something, the salesperson can ask them a question or give them feedback on their update.

Send a private Twitter, Facebook, or LinkedIn message to them congratulating them on a recent success, trip or personal achievement. It could be as simple as, "Amazing photos of your trip to London! How long were you there?"

Say thank-you, all the time, to everyone (if possible), and then follow-up with a personalized comment or question. For instance, a client or prospect clicks "like" on an article from Forbes that the salesperson happened to share on LinkedIn. In the comments section they could tag them and say, "Thanks Paul! What did you like about the study by Harvard on Emotional Intelligence?" Or if someone follows them on Twitter or shares/retweets their content they could say, "Thanks for the follow @PaulSmith – how are things in London?"

These simple but contextual and customized interactions create an emotional tie and memory. People feel recognized and the back-and-forth dialogue often creates the rapport required to allow you to take the next step and engage them at a deeper level in-person, on the phone, or through web conferencing/Skype.

Personalization in conversations can be highly powerful for brands to establish relationships and loyalty with existing customers. On a recent trip across Canada,

Shane Gibson's flight with Air Canada was delayed and then replaced with a different plane – with no new seat assignment for Shane. In a somewhat frantic and frustrated state he went to Twitter to express his frustration, tagging Air Canada, he also noted that he had a keynote speech to deliver in less than 48 hours in another city, and then several other cities to visit after that. Within minutes Air Canada directly messaged Shane on Twitter, asked him for his reservation number.

Shortly after the direct message exchange there was an announcement over the PA that asked Shane to come to the front gate where he was boarded and upgraded to business class. With no prompting Shane of course posted to Twitter and his 37,000+ Twitter followers, that he was grateful that they helped him get on his way. One could argue that this is rather standard practice for a brand but then Air Canada went the extra mile - two days later Air Canada Twitter team reached out to Shane through the direct message and simply said, "Enjoy your flight home Shane!" This doesn't seem like a big deal, but a little extra follow-up can make the customer feel like they're more than a number or a Twitter/Instagram avatar to a brand.

Customer service in this case with @AirCanada was a very public conversation. That public conversation or complaint becomes part of our brand as many people witness and experience the conversation as it unfolds. Seeing it as an opportunity to engage and deepen loyalty and relationships is a form of thought leadership.

IT'S NOT B2B OR B2C DIGITAL COMMUNICATIONS IT'S P2P (PERSON TO PERSON)

The true power of social media isn't the one-to-many aspect, people get excited about having more followers or connections on social networks so that they can post something so that many people can read it. We've heard people refer to their Twitter accounts as Twitter cannons or a large influencer on Instagram talking about posting a video to their Instagram firehose. This evokes images of blasting content out to thousands of people; it misses one of the greatest opportunities in social media marketing and social selling. It's not about B2B or B2C broadcasting, it's about P2P interaction. P2P of course means person to person, it's not about blasting our message out to a bunch of people it's about creating great one-to-one interactions with numerous stakeholders and overtime building deep true relationships or in many cases brand advocates - by taking the time to engage people uniquely and individually.

If we spent 20 minutes each day interacting with just one client or potential client in our online community to deepen the relationship, it can pay big dividends over time. This could be a back and forth dialogue in a Messenger chat, a reply to one of their Instagram updates or tweets, or even a quick thank you for them sharing some great content and then re sharing it for them. They may be in search of advice or insights and we take the time to help that individual by forwarding some information to them and connecting them with someone who's relevant in the marketplace who can help them with their challenge.

These little individual interactions don't seem like a big deal for a large brand, but if that brand did that with one person a day 365 days a year, that brand would have 365 true advocates and fans within their community. Talk to a social media brand manager for a major corporation and ask them who the top 300 influencers are who impact the reach and goodwill of their brand online and most of them will tell you that the list is much shorter than 300. They will admit that they haven't strategically invested in new relationships on a daily basis.

A few years back Shane attended the Guerrilla Marketing Reunion, in Orlando FL. Shane and over 30 other Guerilla Marketing coauthors got together and shared their guerrilla marketing insights at the conference. Seth Godin happens to be one of the original coauthors of Jay Conrad Levinson in the Guerilla Marketing series of books. At that event Seth shared from stage some very sage advice on the true power of community building and social media marketing success. What he said was:

> *"It doesn't scale because we tell the world, it scales because if we treat five people so well, they will tell other people, and they will tell 5 and those become 20 and that's when it scales."*

> - SETH GODIN

Social Conversation Tip: Resist the temptation to over-automate, there are lots of software solutions that will fake authenticity inserting the name of the person saying something like "Dear [insert name] thanks for connecting here on Twitter/ LinkedIn, have a great day!" Anyone who has been on social media for more than a week knows these are disingenuous boiler plated messages. They say to the prospect "you're not important and I couldn't be bothered to learn about you and send a personalized message."

GREAT THOUGHT LEADERS ARE COMMUNITY BUILDERS:

Most successful businesspeople give back to their community. They are continually expanding their network while deepening relationships with their connections. When you don't feel like you have enough, you tend to give very little to other people. This attitude feeds a downward spiral in sales and business. To get, you must first genuinely give value.

Very simply, give more than your competitors think is necessary and connect deeper and more often than your competitors are comfortable with. On giving more: if your competitors share a sound bite daily then share a full blog post or report. If they require an email address, phone number, and an opt-in to get business information then ideally you should make your information or insights available with one click.

If your competitors generically send thank-you's via Twitter, then you should take the time to read about the person and customize a response. "Thanks for the share, how are things in Austin Texas?" is a lot more powerful than "Thanks for the share!"

If your content is truly great and your intent is good you won't need to trick or manipulate people into giving up their contact information – they will come find you.

If you owned a wealth management firm an example of building community may be organizing an event or webinar with a guest speaker on "How to Grow Your Businesses during Tough Economic Times." This event isn't specifically about your products or services, it tackles a topic with broad importance that is bigger than any one financial product. It pulls like-minded people together from your community (and target market). You can record this event on video and audio or stream it live online. You can repurpose this content in the form of reports, short videos, podcasts, transcripts, slide decks, or free online learning for your target market.

A technology MSP (Managed Service Provider) could host an event where they bring in a cybersecurity expert and an ecommerce expert who share with the MSP's local clients and potential clients how they can secure their business and expand their economic opportunities through ecommerce. While the MSP may sell numerous products and solutions that will help them to do this, the webinar is not about that, it's about helping their market and community be more profitable. If they enabled the local business owners to network in breakout groups or talk about their own business briefly, they are also able to add an element of community building or networking. They're not just bringing together experts but actually bringing together like-minded people, in this case small business owners, who can develop closer bonds with other small business owners. This is what real community building is about; it's about doing things bigger than our brand that grows the capacity and the size of our community.

The power of community building as a brand is that you eventually aren't just part of the community, you're the hub of the community. Once you're the hub of a community you're almost a gatekeeper. This is where things get exciting because other people begin to knock on the gate and ask for access to the community. These could be partners and potential collaborators who you can bring into the community to add value but also profit to your bottom line.

Shane Gibson met Avi Arya at the Sociable! book launch in Vancouver in 2009 same year Avi launched Internet Moguls. 10 years later with 240+ employees and global digital agency Avi and his team have worked with some of the world's biggest brands, thought leaders, and celebrities.

His company Internet Moguls digital agency specialized in helping large brands leverage digital for growth and was focused on hotels, restaurants, travel companies, airlines, and tourism boards. When COVID-19 hit South East Asia it sidelined most of their clients.

Before the lockdown Avi promised his audience on social media that Internet Moguls would do a webinar a week starting the 1st of January 2020. Then he was suddenly forced to shut his office down and send over 200 moguls (staff) home. He however did this with the intent of keeping his promise and set up a webinar studio in his home and did 75 webinars in 75 days.

"We had no idea on how and how fast to react and I as the founder had no precedence to follow, teams panicked and wanted to get back to normal ASAP and the only thing I was certain about was that what was then, may never come back again."

By untethering himself and his team from their physical offices, Avi was about to go through an accelerated digital transformation by shifting and redeveloping their business model. That single decision to continue to stay in touch with clients and prospective clients via webinar platforms led to over 700 daily attendees and the momentum built fast, they were doing 3 webinars a day on some days.

The results were significant they grew their email subscribers by 136,000 people and their combined Instagram and Facebook by over 100,000 people. In 75 days Avi and his team achieved growth levels that previously took years. His largest webinar audience was 3200 people.

Avi developed a new sales and marketing process that helped convert many people and companies in this large community to online workshop and course customers. He re-launched into the tourism and hospitality space using the webinar marketing sales funnel to sell new digital marketing programs and solutions that were relevant for today's virtual economy.

"We now we have a much leaner team much smaller office and a bigger client list, most importantly a way more rewarding a lifestyle than ever before for me and my time. We work yet take frequent breaks and take time off when we want to, we started cycling and health focused activities. Being a virtual company now allows us to say yes to global opportunities and deliver through a talent pool of Global Pivoters, while maintaining a healthy work/life balance.

I call this the 2030 life and I urge everybody reading this book to adopt this
the new world order, a space in which you can sell
any product or service to any customer in any part of the world
from the beach watching your kids play and sipping a
beer while compromising on NOTHING."

– AVI ARYA

The key take-away of these examples is this that great Thought Leaders find ways to galvanize their community and target market through giving and leading. They look for ways to help community members with their business, career, and personal life. It may be something as simple as sharing a local charities fundraiser on Twitter or something as involved as organizing an online web series of local business experts that can help your target clients. The keyword here is *contribution*.

ONCE YOU HAVE BUILT A COMMUNITY - AMPLIFY YOUR MESSAGE THROUGH IT:

One of our favorite leadership quotes comes from John C. Maxwell and he states, "One is too few a number to achieve greatness." This is a foundational social communications and social selling truth. To build a powerful presence and reputation you need a community that trusts you. You may never have the celebrity of the CEO of a major tech start-up BUT you can build alliances with those CEOs.

Genuine relationships with people will give you leverage for your message and your mission. Invest in building relationships with the communities and influencers that can help amplify your personal brand and give you access to networks beyond your company's circle of influence.

Social Selling Tip: Timing is everything in social selling. Resist the temptation to "close" someone on a meeting or phone call right away. Spend time sharing great content, contributing to their success, and having great conversations. Once this foundation is laid then asking for a meeting or initial phone call often feels natural for your sales team.

We have put together a list of 30 key actions you need to be taking consistently to be a Thought Leader in your chosen markets and communities. Beside each action rate yourself from 1 to 5, 1 being no or never and 5 being yes or always. A score of 2 or 3 would mean you are somewhat doing the activity or inconsistently doing it.

Content	1	2	3	4	5	Total
We are on all of the major social networks our clients and customers are						
We produce 3-5 great pieces of content a week as a minimum						
We have a content calendar we follow						
We leverage all mediums including articles, videos, images, audio, etc.						
We produce content that is designed for specific stages in the sales cycle						
We encourage our sales team to create and curate content on their own						
We encourage team members to share our content						
We curate valuable content from other sources and share it						
We focus our content on helping our target market reach their goals						
We produce reports, how-to's, and guides distributing them broadly online						
Total Score for Content:						/50
Conversation	1	2	3	4	5	
We have identified where and when and in what form our Nanotribes converse online						
We understand the communications etiquette of each platform and medium we are using						
We understand the culture, values and communications nuances of out Nanotribes						
We invite customer comments proactively on platforms like Twitter, Instagram, and LinkedIn						
We reply to customer comments online quickly						
We have social media guidelines and training that guide but don't hamper online conversations						
We look for opportunities to engage and comment on community posts and content						
We customize and personalize our comments and conversations						
We use social search tools to monitor conversations across multiple platforms						
We use conversations to build value and establish rapport not pitch or push						
Total Score for Conversation:						/50

Community	1	2	3	4	5	
We are proactively growing our following and connections daily in our chosen social networks						
We are following the 80/20 rule – 80% value added activity and 20% marketing and promotion						
We seek out and invite people into the community that build and help the community						
We create opportunities for like-minded people to connect, collaborate, and grow together						
We use we use our social clout and influence to champion important community causes and initiatives						
We are proactively building an inclusive and diverse online community and network						
We empower individual employees to be community builders and value-added influencers in the community						
We model high ethical standards, positivity in messaging, and a giving ethos						
We collaborate with other Thought Leaders and communities on projects that will grow and add value to our respective networks						
We constantly looking for new and relevant platforms and networks to find and grow our community on						
Total Score for Community:						/50

Content _____ + Conversation _____ + Community _____ = _____/150
(Thought Leadership Score)
Results interpretation:

30 – 50   You likely have no real thought leadership in the marketplace. Time to put a plan in place and take action. A score this low means many potential clients don't know you exist or understand your relevance. You're marketing like it's 1999.

51- 80   Your competitors are most likely out-shining you. Your online presence meets the bare minimum in today's virtual economy. Very few people online would be able to determine or learn about your expertise.

81-100   You have some momentum in establishing yourself as an online Thought Leader. Likely your organization has neglected one of your three Thought Leadership categories (Content, Conversation, or Community). Focus on bringing up your lowest scoring area and double down on the one that you have momentum in.

101-125 You have a solid brand as a Thought Leader with a vibrant growing community. Inbound leads and opportunities should be happening as a result. To level up you will likely need to invest in more people and resources to reach your full potential. If you haven't already written a strategic plan for your Thought Leadership, time to get one in place.

126-150 Congratulations! If you're not already dominating your chosen niche and Nanotribes as the go-to Thought Leader you will be soon. Keep up the momentum and continue to invest in your team, social media marketing strategy, and insights. (In fact, contact us! We want to hear your story.)

5 STAGES OF CONSENT IN SOCIAL SELLING

According to a recent study by JD Power and Associates the average consumer has completed 80% of the buying cycle before they reach out and engage a car dealership for the first time. Much of their research and evaluation happens silently or without triggering any awareness on behalf of the automotive manufacturer or dealerships. Depending on your industry your customer will on average have completed somewhere between 60% and 90% of the buying cycle before you even know they exist. At that point they will fill out a form, register for a webinar, or maybe begin to chat with one of your chatbots online. If you're not active on social media and investing in your thought leadership it's likely that many of your competitors have been educating your customer with their content, conversations, and community actions. Your goal is to understand the five stages of consent in social selling and to proactively invest in thought leadership activities that are relevant for each step so that you can catch the interest and awareness of your ideal customers well before they move down the sales funnel or through their buying process.

Consent to sell or permission-based marketing is a vital component of successful social selling. The 5 Stages of Consent are in essence your online social sales funnel, they're all the things that happen to take the prospect from being a stranger to becoming a warm receptive lead or friend. (Shane originally developed these 5 Stages of Consent when he collaborated with his late friend and mentor Jay Conrad Levinson on their book, "Guerrilla Social Media Marketing.") There's an old idiom that says, "no one likes to be sold but everyone likes to buy." This sums up what consent is about; consent is about someone giving you permission to help facilitate them through their buying process. It's not about a pitch or a landing page video where you've trapped them and are pushing them into making an urgent decision. When someone gives you consent to market or sell to them it's truly a collaborative relationship-oriented sale or transaction. Let's take a look at each of these five steps and talk about how you can capitalize on them within your sales and marketing team.

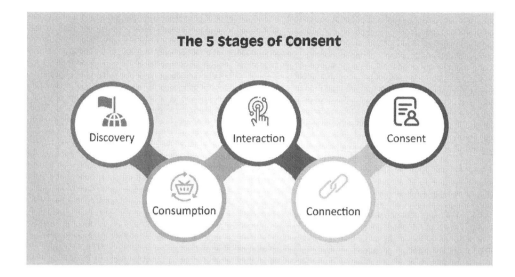

The 5 Stages of Consent

Discovery — Interaction — Consent — Consumption — Connection

STEP 1 – DISCOVERY:

Discovery is the first thing that needs to happen in your online social sales funnel. This may happen when you pro-actively search for prospects on LinkedIn or Twitter and engage them. In many cases you are discovered reactively; your prospect may hear your name tweeted several times by their community. Possibly, they discover you through a local Google listing you filled out or they came to your website through a keyword Google search. This step is about finding the right connections and being found by the right connections. Being Discoverable is vital, your online social graph (what people find when they search for you or your business) is now your business card. Here are a few questions you may want to ask yourself about your discoverability:

1) What do people see when they search for you or your business in Google?

2) Is your website and LinkedIn profile well optimized for keywords related to your industry that people search for?

3) Do you know the most popular keywords used by your target market to find businesses like yours on Google, Amazon, LinkedIn, etc. and are you using that data well?

4) Are key staff being interviewed or profiled by leading podcasters, bloggers, YouTube influencers, or local news sites?

5) Are all of your employees LinkedIn profiles up-to-date and connected to your business page?

6) Are you creating, curating, and sharing content that resonates with your key Nanotribes continually to increase your chances of being discovered?

7) Have you created a local listing on Google Places?
(https://www.google.com/business/)

8) Have you listed your business on regional directories and community sites?

9) Do you have an up-to-date profile on the major social media platforms including LinkedIn, Facebook, Twitter, and depending on your market Instagram?

10) Are you hosting webinars or leveraging other platforms that bring the community together?

11) Are you listing any relevant products or services on ecommerce platforms or marketplaces to increase visibility?

12) Are you organizing or participating in online conferences, webinars, or events that will increase your exposure to new communities and markets?

13) Is your business and team reserving profile names on new and emerging social media networks?

If you answered yes to at least 5 of these questions you're on your way to being discoverable. If not… you're likely your own best kept secret.

Social Discovery Tip: Discovery can happen in-person when you hand someone a card with your blog, Twitter, or LinkedIn profile on it. It could happen via publicity you have garnered, through advertising or even from delivering a webinar for your local Chamber of Commerce. When people discover you offline make sure they can easily learn about your online presence.

STEP 2 - CONSUMPTION:

Now that you have been discovered your prospective customer or client will begin to consume the content you create. Too many people at this point immediately spring into action, pitching their visitors or new connections with offers, and various other types of Me Marketing (My book, my download, my product, etc.) You need to give your content and community time to help build your credibility and warm up the prospect.

This is where content quality and relevancy is vital. If you have taken the time to create and curate content that truly appeals to your Nanotribes, then they will stick around, and consume it. Many will even share it with their connections. Even an interaction with the customer online can be consumed by other members of the community as that interaction is a public activity, a Twitter thread or a back and forth answer on Instagram is content and can make us discoverable.

Denis recently commented on a LinkedIn post of a client of his, he made a remark about how much he enjoyed working with them, they replied and affirmed that they enjoyed it as well. That same day another executive from an organization associated with the first one reached out to Denis and let him know that he wanted to learn more about what he did for his client. That comment quickly turned into an interaction and then consent to sell to a new prospective client who is now doing business with Denis. In fact, the new client then referred Denis to another person who is now a new client. High quality conversations are high-quality content – these conversations can be found, read (consumed), and drive interaction long after they have been posted.

Find ways to exceed the community's expectations with high-value content. This is where the quality and variety of your writing, the value of your studies and white papers, and even the entertainment factor in your videos, all become vital.

Vital beats viral in social media marketing and social selling. Viral content is catchy and shareable, but it doesn't build trust and credibility like content that is vital to the success or survival of your clients and customers.

Some of the most effective content today is deep content (Whitepapers, Reports, In-depth webinars, etc.) but it's a mistake to only produce content that requires a large commitment. Use micro or popcorn content to seed the marketplace and drive people to your deeper content. With that said, streaming real-time video on YouTube, LinkedIn, and Facebook as well as archives of past shows are continuing to be effective means of consumption and engagement.

> **Vital beats viral in social media marketing and social selling. Viral content is catchy and shareable, but it doesn't build trust and credibility like content that is vital to the success or survival of your clients and customers.**

You gain consent by being trustworthy, trust is based upon credibility. For some people if they read two of your blog posts they like, they may sign up for your email newsletter, and send you a quick tweet or LinkedIn message. Other people may read your blog for six months, follow your Instagram updates, and lurk about on Facebook observing you before you ever know they're there. Being active daily and using multiple social media channels will ensure that your prospects can consume the information they want in the format they want for as long as they need to. This consumption will often lead to an interaction, where the prospect you don't know hits your radar.

STEP 3 - INTERACTION:

Interaction can happen in several ways. Sometimes you can jump right to the interaction stage if the timing is right, other times it can take a while before you can engage. If someone on Twitter or LinkedIn asked a question about the difference between two different products you sell on your ecommerce site, it is most likely this person would be open to you interacting with them and giving them answers almost right away. If they are talking about a general business topic on LinkedIn it might not be the right context for a conversation about what you're selling online.

Interaction can also occur by you being proactive and visiting the social profiles of your target market and making value-added comments and starting conversations. Another form of Interaction is customer-driven, where after consuming our content they begin to make comments or even simply "like" the update. All of these are door-openers to the next stage of relationship development.

Social Selling Tip: The "Interaction" phase is the "conversation" strategy we talked about in Thought Leadership. This doesn't stop once someone becomes a client or a friend. Keeping the conversation going is vital to deepen relationships and increase revenues from our clients.

STEP 4 - CONNECTION:

"If content is king then connection is queen."

When someone connects with our company on Facebook or LinkedIn, they are allowing us to see more of their world, their business, and their personality. This helps us customize and adjust our sales and communications to match their needs and values.

"Connection is the doorway to consent – but it is not consent"

Connection is mistaken by many salespeople as consent to pitch and sell. A connection can be when someone adds a person as a friend on Facebook, a connection on LinkedIn, or mutually follows them on Twitter. They could follow your company page on LinkedIn or Facebook as well. In the world of online dating, it would be the equivalent of accepting a connection on Tinder; you haven't agreed to go on a date, you have just agreed to learn more about each other. A connection can also be signing up for your newsletter or blog updates via email.

At this point don't push marketing messages, special offers, and all those other types of Me Marketing at them. Help them learn more about your organization – in many cases they don't want to buy from you yet. This is an important credibility-building stage and is often where "lead nurturing" starts – this is where you can begin to proactively push your blog posts, whitepapers, and videos, etc. to them via email or other private messaging tools. We would strongly suggest personalizing your messages for your top 20% of prospects and semi-automating your less ideal opportunities.

HOW IMPORTANT IS LEAD NURTURING? (FREQUENT VALUE-ADDED PROACTIVE TOUCHES)

Lead nurturing is perpetual and will continue for as long as your relationship exists, it doesn't live in the front of your sales funnel. It's an attitude and a sense of curiosity around how you can deepen relationships with your key prospects and accounts. It's not just about scheduling an interaction weekly with a prospect or group of prospects, it's about asking, "How can we be of immense value to the individuals in our Nanotribes every week? What can I share with them that helps achieve this goal?" Here are some interesting stats on why lead nurturing or frequency selling is important in this process:

*"Nurtured leads produce, on average, a 20% increase
in sales opportunities versus non-nurtured leads."*

- DEMANDGEN REPORT

*According to Forrester Research: companies that excel at lead nurturing
generate 50% more sales leads at 33% lower cost per lead.*

The bottom-line is lead nurturing creates more sales and those sales are generally larger than non-nurtured leads. One of the important areas where sales and marketing need to align is in the creation of digital sales enablement content. It's great to tell your tenured sales professional that they need to share great content at every step in the sales funnel and even after the sale. This is a true statement but it's also a lot of work to do it well and consistently.

How your marketing team can support the sales team at being more effective with lead nurturing is to develop engaging content, reports, video, and other relevant types of content for your target market. It's important to note that the type of content someone will consume and find valuable while they are in the discovery phase or consideration phase of the buying process is completely different than the type of content they will find useful when they are at the step of making a final decision or reviewing a proposal for instance. Here's a quick process you can follow to map out what type of content you need to create to support your sales team in driving a solid lead nurturing program.

1) First define your top Nanotribes and specific market segments that your sales team is targeting.

2) Once your key segments are defined map out the unique buying process steps or sales process steps that your prospects will move through in each group.

3) List the types of questions, concerns, or information that will be needed by your prospect in each stage respectively.

4) Take into consideration the fact that there are usually five to six buyers influencing a corporate purchase, make sure that your content appeals to these multiple personas within a target company. Your thought leadership content or lead nurturing pieces will be different for a senior level executive than a mid-level executive or a frontline purchasing decision maker.

5) Brainstorm the types of content you could create that would help your sales team establish rapport, build credibility, educate the customer, and move them to the next step in the sales or buying cycle.

6) Put a project plan in place to produce the needed content for each of these key sales funnels, remember to vary the types of mediums, formats, and depth of content so that your sales team has some flexibility in the way they run their lead nurturing process.

7) Organize the content so it is easily accessible from your CRM and organized based upon the target vertical and stage of the sales process so that your sales team can easily find it and share it.

8) Lastly keep your lead nurturing program fresh by sending out a weekly digest of new social content and organize it by market type and stage of the sales cycle so that your sales team can easily share new social content that you've created. You can use a tool like PostBeyond to help organize the social sharing of relevant content.

Your customer success, customer experience, and customer retention teams will be a great source to have ideas for content creation in your sales enablement process. The reason why is they can tell you what misinformation or lack of insights the customers may have that is led to customer experience and service challenges. You can use this business intelligence to create content they can be shared earlier on in the sales cycle to mitigate some of these customer service and customer success challenges.

You can think about investing in customer nurturing content that can help improve the success of the implementation of your solutions, their experience, and overall customer satisfaction just like you do with the sales team with the sales enablement content.

STEP 5 - CONSENT:

> *"If relationships are currency,*
> *then consent would be the gold standard."*
>
> – JAY CONRAD LEVINSON, AUTHOR OF GUERRILLA MARKETING

Many sales professionals spend a lot of time gaining customers but neglect to truly build relationships and therefore miss long-term opportunities. On the other hand, there are a lot of social media marketers who have thousands of followers, blog readers, and friends but don't have consent to market or sell to them.

Consent separates good social salespeople and marketers who make things happen from those who sit back and hope things happen.

HOW AND WHEN DOES CONSENT HAPPEN?

- You have consent when someone has agreed to subscribe to your newsletter and given you their email address for that purpose.
- Consent can happen in the form of a question or inquiry over Twitter or Instagram when someone asks you a specific question about a service you offer or a product you sell.
- When someone attends a free webinar by your company there's an implied consent to share an offer or a call to action providing the webinar has truly great content.
- Offline connections, where someone you meet tells you they want to learn more about your business, is a form of consent.
- When an inbound lead fills out an information request form or downloads a whitepaper and agrees to receive offers and updates.

Great social salespeople and social media marketers love this level of permission so much that they are careful to respect boundaries. They keep a good ratio of high-value lead nurturing content and interaction to pitching and offers. We would suggest an 80/20 mix where at least 80% of your content and conversations are helpful and value added and 20% are marketing or sales orientated messaging. This marketing and messaging must be in the context of that individual or Nanotribes core needs, values, and situation.

It's important to note that there are varying degrees and types of consent. The prospect could ask us to do one or more of the following:

- Sell to me
- Educate me
- Stay in touch
- Build a relationship

When we think about content and lead nurturing it's important to develop specific lead nurturing strategies based upon the type of consent we have.

Beyond the initial sale, our goal is to continue to develop greater levels of intimacy through value added Thought Leadership. Gaining a profitable loyal customer is expensive, and strong relationships are the insurance that protects that investment. If nurtured properly, those relationships can pay year after year in the form of direct purchases, as well as referrals. This builds wallet-share and expands the breadth of products and services they use.

GETTING SOCIABLE TO DRIVE SALES RESULTS:

Social media is not a video game or a popularity contest, especially for salespeople who are responsible for generating revenues. When Shane Gibson wrote "Sociable!" with Stephen Jagger the title of the book represented the need to go deeper and get real with our online connections. Being Sociable! is about using the internet to get off of the internet and connect in person (or to at least deepen the engagement past that). Very few things drive more ROI from social selling activities than old-fashioned one-on-one meetings. When we connect with someone on Twitter or LinkedIn our intent is to eventually meet them face-to-face, and if that's not possible then do a Skype Video, Zoom, or Google Hangout.

When one-on-one you quickly learn the truth about a person and an opportunity. Once someone has met you in person, they will most likely trust you more and pay more attention to your online activities as well. Make it a goal to connect weekly with at least one online connection and take them offline (or onto a video call). This one activity will accelerate sales cycles and build trust fast.

A DAY IN THE LIFE OF A SOCIAL SELLING SELLER:

As a sales leader, business owner, or sales professional it's important to understand the reality of successful social selling. Social selling is not just about thought leadership, and it's definitely not about scrolling through Facebook and LinkedIn several hours a day. Great social salespeople are proactive prospector's, consistent publishers, and have a set of daily KPIs (key performance indicators) that they commit to completing and achieving.

Shane Gibson in partnership with the Canadian Professional Sales Association reached out to their members and asked them to participate in a questionnaire and study that looked at quota attainment rates and social media use by sales professionals for sales purposes. Several hundred opted in to do the questionnaire and study sharing their quota attainment results of the previous year as well as their social media use and habits.

One of the interesting results that came out of the study was the fact that 50% of sales professionals that did not use social media as part of their sales process missed the quota. In contrast, less than 9% of salespeople who use social media for sales missed the quota. The surprise was:

"Sales professionals that used social media 1-3 times per day outperformed those that didn't use social media at all or used social media 5+ times per day for sales purposes."

At first, after analyzing the data, they thought it was a mistake, it seemed counterintuitive that using social media 1-3 times per day outperformed using it five or more times per day. Here was the big finding:

"At some point social networking can become social notworking, this is where we overuse the tool, neglect other important sales activities, and ultimately lose grip of reality and what's important in our day-to-day sales activities."

The key to success in social selling isn't about creating one glorious viral video that makes you famous or writing literary masterpieces for LinkedIn articles. It's about simple, effective, daily activities that are measured and strategic in nature. It's about committing to be proactively engaged in social sales for at least 30 minutes twice per day.

Here's the kind of manageable regiment we would suggest every salesperson commits to daily:

1. Check for signals (email opens, likes, retweets, comments, private messages).

2. Visit "top client / top prospect" profiles for updates and opportunities to engage.

3. Look for trigger/life events on LinkedIn, Facebook, Instagram, and Twitter.

4. Thank / follow-back / connect with new connections.

5. Add offline connections you meet to LinkedIn, Instagram, Twitter, etc.

6. Curate or create 1-2 pieces of great content daily.

7. Ask for introductions on LinkedIn, Facebook, and Twitter.

8. Do something community focused (give back, participate in something, share something, etc.)

9. Engage with key influencers of your Nanotribes and the greater community as a whole.

10. Send content to key accounts for lead nurturing as prompted by the CRM.

These 10 daily steps when applied consistently will help build major momentum and community. It seems like a lot initially but once you are set-up and rolling it becomes second nature. Tying this all together using a CRM and even a sales workflow tool like Salesloft can keep us organized and efficient. The one common thread of most successful social sellers is that they are consistently applying the basics on a daily basis, that consistency will outperform a competitor who infrequently posts great content but isn't present on a daily basis in the key social networks that are vital to their target market.

LEVERAGING ECOMMERCE AND PLATFORM THINKING

Another aspect of addressing the digitally fragmented marketplace is the need to leverage ecommerce tools and platforms. While we spent a large portion of this book talking about the power of building a virtual sales team of right-brained sales leaders, there's a parallel reality: salespeople are being replaced by ecommerce sites, apps, and platforms. Part of being a successful brand and sales organization is being an omnichannel and omni-platform thinker. It's not Amazon versus your own hosted ecommerce site or deciding whether or not you need to leverage in-app shopping on Instagram... it's all of the above for most organizations. The key is to understand which channel(s) your existing and future customers are on and developing a multi-channel approach.

Ecommerce was already on a meteoric rise before the pandemic forced people back into their homes and online to shop for the things they need and want. Depending upon your source, ecommerce experts and research organizations have estimated that in 2020 we experienced growth that was expected to take until 2028 or possibly 2030 to happen. In the US alone in the first two quarters of 2020 consumers spent $347.26 billion online up 30.1% from $266.84 billion for the same period in 2019. That is a 230% greater growth rate compared to the same period in 2019 which saw a 12.1 % growth in ecommerce.

Amazon represents almost a third of all US ecommerce revenues. This is an important thing to note because Amazon is truly a platform not unlike Netflix, Uber, or Alibaba. They have combined the power of ecommerce with platform thinking. The massive growth in ecommerce also made Jeff Bezos the wealthiest person in history at a personal net worth of $193.5 Billion (at the time of writing this book). Amazon surpassed 150 million Prime Members up from 100 million in 2018.

What's important to note is that the US is only a fraction of the potential opportunity that ecommerce channels present. Having consumers and business decision makers shift to online purchasing and ecommerce platforms means that your physical location is less important and who purchases from you and where they are located may change drastically in the virtual economy.

"96 percent of all of the world's consumers and over three-quarters of the world's purchasing power are outside of the United States"

- LINDA MCMAHON, HEAD OF THE U.S. SMALL BUSINESS ADMINISTRATION

One trend we are seeing as trainers, speakers, and consultants is an uptick in organizations that are located in other countries that are finding us and engaging us to deliver live and pre-recorded digital content. In the past, many conference organizers and corporations would try to find a local speaker or trainer for their event or their training program. Today thanks to Google, YouTube, LinkedIn, and our books on Amazon we can be discovered by a larger audience, and we can spend a lot less time traveling to go deliver our solutions and programs to clients around the world.

It's important to define and expand the context of what most people think of ecommerce is. When we think ecommerce we think of books, clothing, household items, food, and other physical products delivered to the consumer. This is truly only a portion of the types of products and services that are sold leveraging ecommerce technology. Digital products such as software, apps, online courses, eBooks, and conference tickets to virtual conferences are sold by ecommerce. A consultant delivering online live video-based work to their clients would be considered an ecommerce business model if the clients can subscribe to or pay for those services through that person's website or a third-party platform digitally.

Ecommerce is driven by mobile, in addition to this digital commerce and digital networks not only drive ecommerce revenues but drive a significant amount of retail or bricks and mortar revenues as well. Your presence on ecommerce platforms and social networks will drive your offline business.

"...more than **62% of ecommerce traffic now comes from mobile** devices. The share of **orders placed over mobile** devices is increasing rapidly too, **growing 41% year over year**…. (and) more than 50% of retail commerce still happens in physical stores. Influencing more than 50% of that in-store commerce, however, is the digital environment—from multiple channels (social media, blogs, online retail) and multiple devices (mobile phones, tablets, computers)." - Salesforce.com

A growing trend that continues to pick up speed is the combination or bundling of physical and digital products. A variation of this is when a company that provides a tangible service such as consulting begins to bundle that with digital products such as membership sites, custom software solutions, or even physical products.

A fitness coach that's doing remote classes may build an online store where their clients can access fitness related products such as stretch bands, yoga mats, weights, and even white labeled supplements that can be delivered to the home of their customers and clients. This coach could even create a subscription model where for a monthly fee their customers get access to their live online courses plus a standing order of supplements and a premium fitness box full of products that will help the person improve their fitness. This combination of physical products, digital subscriptions, and live interaction is a great example of how we can blend ecommerce into an existing successful business model to make it more engaging for the customer and increase the lifetime value and monthly spend of customers.

Lululemon recently bought Mirror which is an in-home fitness company for the purchase price of 500 million dollars. Mirror is literally a digital mirror that you hang on your wall, when it's turned off it's simply a three quarter length mirror, when you turn it on it becomes an interactive home gym with instruction engagement and courses that include weekly live classes, on-demand workouts as well as access to one-on-one personal training.

This is an interesting ecommerce play for Lululemon - this is a way they can truly enhance their ecommerce presence while expanding recurring revenues and growing the Mirror customer base significantly through their own marketing channels and customer base. This is a bold step and shows some real innovation, not only is Lululemon able to offer and get access to these digital customers to sell physical products, they're actually going to own an ecommerce screen in the home of their customers. This type of creative bold thinking is the type of thinking we all need to apply to our businesses in this new virtual economy.

Digital products and selling software related services are some of the highest margin ecommerce offerings that you could add to your existing business (or new business model). This is your opportunity to move into the digital product space and tap into a monthly recurring revenue model that could change and scale your business. Your digital products give you more frequent engagement as your customer interacts with your brand multiple times per day.

Jay McBain, Principal Analyst - Channels, Partnerships and Ecosystems - for Forrester Research recently shared some interesting insights during a keynote delivered for ChannelNext Virtual, a monthly virtual conference for technology MSPs and Software Vendors. He shared with us that in Canada 81% of CPA (Accounting) firms are converting their business model to be focused on providing tech services. These are traditional professional services organizations that are pivoting to become tech companies that deliver accounting services driven by technology.

Many of these firms will either resell other people's technology solutions or in many cases develop some of their own subscription based financial software solutions for their client base, these may be in the form of mobile apps or cloud-based solutions that integrate with Salesforce.com or another leading business platform.

What we'd like you to think about is how can you productize what you have in a way that enables you to drive online transactions creating more consistent revenue and helping you find and service new markets. We encourage you to challenge yourself to start thinking like a tech company or a digital-first virtual enterprise by asking yourself these questions:

- How can you start truly transacting with your customers online to deliver physical products and/or services?
- What products or services that you already offer could be packaged or bundled in a way that could be sold through your own ecommerce site or through a third-party platform?
- What type of digital products or services could you create that can enhance your relationship with your existing customer base or open up a new market for you entirely?

- Are there existing software companies out there where you could be reselling their solutions? Ideally, this would allow you to add on your existing products or services to offer an enhanced solution?
- How could you transition in-person or retail purchases and transactions online and in a way that adds value to the customer?

For many organizations wanting to do business via ecommerce it's important to note that most fail before they get started. The failure rate for new ecommerce ventures is 90% after 120 days according to a recent survey by MarketingSignals. One thing that is important to note is why those businesses or ecommerce ventures failed. The biggest contributing factor: "Poor online marketing performance coupled with an overall lack of search engine visibility."

Ecommerce is much more of a science than an art, and your success often comes down to understanding your numbers, logistics, and how key advertising and marketing platforms work (and how to optimize them). Additionally, the reviews and voice of the customer are critical to your long-term success. Shane Facilitates a program for the World Trade Centre Vancouver called ICE (Integrated ecommerce Essentials).

This program focuses on helping exporters leverage ecommerce to tap into new markets. Even if you are expanding to an adjacent State or Province the key principles still apply. We thought we would share with you some of the key steps and best practices of organizations that are successfully using ecommerce to grow their businesses nationally and internationally. While there are many processes, tactics, and principles to ecommerce success here are our top 10:

1) **Research, make no assumptions, and know your numbers**: Understand your competition, your target market, and Nanotribes. Adapting to local regulations, politics, and trade barriers before you choose a market is critical. According to BDC (Business Development Bank of Canada), the single biggest factor that impacts your success in a new market is your knowledge of the competitive landscape. You need to know your product or service costs as well as key numbers and ecommerce metrics – if these numbers are off or inaccurate huge gross revenues could mean big losses. Understanding your break-even point, margins, conversion rates, etc. are all vital.

2) **Choose the right platform(s)**: Is it Shopify? Salesforce? Instagram Storefronts? Magento? Woo Commerce and/or Amazon and eBay? If you want to enter China for instance none of these platforms will work (Alibaba has many solutions and partners for you). Some of these tools require you to drive all of the traffic such as your own Shopify based site and others like Amazon have millions of visitors but keep a large chunk of your profit margin. If you're selling digital products like apps or software then you will want to look at platforms like GitHub, Apple's App Store, or Google Play. If it's something like an online course, then you may need to host it or list and host the course on a site like Udemy.

3) **Distribution**: You're unlikely to ship a single consumer item directly to another country or region. You will need some type of 3PL (3rd Party Logistics) partner or system to tap into who can warehouse and distribute locally. If you are shipping directly or need to ship pallets or containers overseas you will also need to ramp up your knowledge of shipping partners and best practices in logistics.

4) **Marketing**: Organic social media marketing, paid social ads, search engine optimization, marketing copy, on-site shopping cart design, and your check-out process are all part of your success. This is a vital area of focus. You need to drive engagement, create traffic, and build a community around your online brand and products. Whatever you spend on designing and launching your site is about 50% of what you will need to spend marketing it in the first few months.

5) **Getting paid**: Your shopping cart ideally will offer multiple currencies. The good ones have little friction in the check-out process. Many leading online retailers offer Apply Pay, WeChat pay, Google Pay, plus Visa, American Express, Mastercard, and in some cases Bitcoin. For instance, in a recent purchase from Partake Brewing, Shane ordered a case of non-alcoholic beer while watching a presenter at a conference. He chose Apple Pay, with one click and verifying his ID with his thumbprint on his phone he bought the items. This was a relatively frictionless process. To increase revenues, you need to find ways to speed up and increase the ease of the checkout process. If your customer has to enter everything manually, one error message can bounce them.

6) **Intellectual property**: Are your trademarks, patents, and copyrights respected in the countries you plan to export to? Spending the extra money to register in those countries before entering will save you a lot of grief in the long run. The same goes for top level domain names in each country.

7) **Taxation compliance**: You need to consult a tax expert before you ship your first order to that exciting new market. For instance, in many states in the USA (but not all), you are still responsible for ensuring that local sales taxes are paid on the goods you sell – even if you have shipped them from another state or country. This tax bill and others like it can accumulate quickly.

8) **Cross-cultural awareness**: Colors (or colours), terminology, greetings, eating habits, social norms, gender issues, national holidays, and religious considerations are all a part of your market entry and on-going marketing, packaging, and service strategy.

9) **Cybersecurity**: Billions of dollars are stolen annually online. If your site is compromised and you lose customer data or payment information, you could be sued for thousands or in some cases millions of dollars of damages. Most small or medium size businesses never recover from a major breach. Invest in a tool like Symantec's Intrusion Prevention System (IPS) to stop hackers from using your ecommerce storefront to compromise your customers. Also engage professionals to protect your own devices and business networks. Later in the book, we will be outlining what you can do to secure your business against these types of threats.

10) **Creativity**: Watch, adapt, and innovate - the online space is evolving faster than ever. Your competitors are likely leveraging tools like Artificial Intelligence to drive marketing and merchandising decisions. New social platforms are gaining traction daily, and memes which are vital to today's marketing change in format and tone rapidly. We need to stay on top of what's happening and invest in learning about what "might happen." Take a risk, try new networks, new marketing tools, or unique marketing partners, and see what can give you the edge.

CHAPTER 8

SELECTING AND LEVERAGING SALES TECHNOLOGY

Selecting and leveraging the right technologies to grow your and future proof your business is a mission critical task. The number of competing solutions all with equally compelling features and client success stories can be overwhelming. We discussed earlier that there are over 5000 SaaS or cloud-based sales technology companies producing one or more sales technology solutions each. Some of them could drastically change the way you sell, improving efficiencies, and creating new opportunities, others are rather novel or are barely out of beta and could possibly distract your team and cost you your business. Your technology choices need to be strategic in nature and implemented correctly to ensure you get the right ROI for your investment and your team's activities.

For the purpose of this chapter, we decided to focus on the type of solutions that support your sales and sales management functions of your business. We're going to present them in the context of what is called technology stacks or tech stacks.

A tech stack is a series of software solutions that work together and are integrated in a way that helps you and your team consistently execute business best practices or a process. Originally the concept of a tech stack comes from the world of computer programming, and in its purest form is a series of tools a team would use to develop, build- out and run a software solution or application. In this chapter when we use the term tech stack, we're focusing on the technology that helps execute specific business processes.

It's important to note that we are not going to give you a shopping list of all the types of software that fall under each category in the sales tech space. This is where we'd like to issue a bit of a disclaimer, we're going to review some of the leading and innovative tools available today but fully expect that many of them will either become redundant, rebrand themselves, or be purchased by a competitor and integrated into their system. What this means is that regardless of what we have to say here you have to do your own research and determine what solutions are best for you in real time.

When Shane wrote Guerrilla Social Media Marketing with Jay Conrad Levinson, they gave their final draft of the book to the publisher in May of that year. By the following October when the book was launched, of the 100+ social media marketing and social sales tools they listed in the book almost 30% of them had either stopped operating, been purchased and integrated into another system or had been eclipsed by a better more innovative platform. This is how fast technology moves. More important than the specific tools, are the process of organizing and evaluating the tech and how it will support your business processes. It's important to constantly audit, evaluate, and evolve our tech stack.

BUILDING YOUR SALES TECH STACK

It's easy to be reactive to our technology. With Shane's sales training company being on the radar of many organizations he literally gets two to three meeting requests per day from sales executives who work for sales software companies that have a new widget, app, or next generation CRM. In the opinion of the salesperson and vendor, Shane and his clients need to urgently use these tools today. Their proof of ROI and how these tools can improve sales processes are pretty compelling, all they want is just a 30-minute initial phone call to do a demo of their software.

Most software solutions come with a free trial and it gets pretty easy to just give them your credit card and try it out for 30 days, and then if you multiply that by four to five solutions a week in no time you could have a collection of sales apps many of which you don't use, and all of which probably weren't purchased strategically. Then of course depending on the size of your organization multiply that by the number of sales teams you have all with different sets of sales technology tools they're using. This is how you could easily have a completely reactive sales technology approach, where you're dependent upon sales professionals from these tech companies reaching out to you telling you that you need their software. Alternatively, you could strategically look at your business and sales processes and develop criteria for what ideal software should look like, and then strategically go out into the marketplace to find the best software that meets your needs.

What becomes dangerous with the ad hoc technology approach is that you have a lot of good client data and insights residing in dozens of software systems that may not be integrated. At the leadership level, this means you do not have access or the visibility of key pieces of customer data and team activities. Let's say for instance, within your organization you're not supporting or paying for LinkedIn Sales Navigator for your sales team but one of your key sales executives decides to pay for it on their own and is not integrated with your CRM. At this point your salesperson starts to live in LinkedIn Sales Navigator because of course, it's a great tool, they have dozens of conversations per day with key clients, prospects, and partners. All of this doesn't get logged into the CRM manually in most cases and when we look at their sales funnel it might appear that they have been inactive or not following up with key clients.

There is a lot of conversation and data that would help other team members understand those clients, that's not available to them. In what is a common worst-case scenario after you've invested a lot of money, time, and corporate resources in this individual, they build a significant pipeline that eventually is going to convert but they quit, go to the competition, or are let go. In all of these scenarios, the hundreds of hours that this person was paid for to build a sales pipeline are lost. The next person that takes over that account executive role won't have access to that pipeline, conversation history, or possibly even the list of prospects. This of course is just a LinkedIn Sales Navigator example, but as we walk you through what a good sales tech stack looks like you're going to be able to see the potential for some serious disorganization, lack of data control, and loss of business intelligence. Just from this perspective it is vital as an organization that we get proactive with the sales technologies that can support our team to be better, invest in the solutions, and ensure that they are integrated and well organized with the proper permissions and policies.

As mentioned in the section of the book on the right-brained sales revolution, today's VP of Sales needs to be one-part leader and one-part CTO. Taking that thought process a step further - if you own your own business and have no director of sales but have a sales team, you or one of your key salespeople need to step in that role. You will need to proactively map out what sales technologies you're going to use to be competitive in the virtual economy. You don't have to be a big business to have a great tech stack, small companies that do what we are advocating can compete with big companies that are slower to adapt.

We're going to go through 11 different categories of sales technology. What we suggest however is that you don't necessarily try to implement and launch eleven categories of software at once. They all have learning curves involved and trying to operate 11 different new types of software at once could be quite daunting. Our suggestion is to pick two or three key pieces, like starting with LinkedIn sales navigator, integrated with a CRM solution, and supported by a prospecting and lead management software like Outreach.io. Once you've put these together and began to master them as a team you can then add other solutions to this core tech stack one at a time - the last thing you want is to have your entire sales team offline for a month not selling while they learn a whole bunch of different software.

We're going to organize your sales tech stack under nine categories, and they are as follows:

1. CRM
2. Lead Generation and Prospecting
3. Contact Enrichment and Intelligence
4. E-mail intelligence and Automation Tools
5. Sales Workflow
6. Communications and Engagement
7. Social Selling
8. Closing
9. Artificial Intelligence

CRM (CUSTOMER RELATIONSHIP MANAGEMENT) SOFTWARE

The first CRM was invented and launched in 1989 by Jon Ferrara, it was called Goldmine, and for those of us who've been in sales that long it's pretty likely that somewhere along the line of your career you've used Goldmine or one of their early competitors such as ACT or Maximizer. CRM has now grown beyond just a place to store your Contacts and send emails from. Depending on which platform and tool you choose you can literally run your entire business from your CRM. Choosing a CRM and implementing it effectively is one of the most critical aspects of managing today's modern and virtual sales force. Sales organizations that aren't using a CRM effectively or no CRM at all are in many cases flying blind and are unlikely to meet their business goals, sales quotas, or even truly understand the lifetime value of their customers or what revenues they're going to generate next quarter. Your CRM will be what the rest of your sales tech stack plugs into (if you pick the right one).

Some CRMs like Salesforce behave more like a platform, where you plug the various aspects of the sales tech stack into them. Salesforce has an entire ecosystem of sales, ecommerce, and business applications tools for all aspects of your business that plug into it, instead of customizing or coding within the CRM to make it unique to you, you're personalizing it by choosing a series of applications produced by 3rd party software companies that are tied together by Salesforce and run the entire workflow of your business. It would be accurate to say that Salesforce is now an operating system for your business more than it is a sales CRM, many of the tools that you can plug into Salesforce make it a Sales CRM tool. Other CRMs like ZOHO CRM are an all-in-one tool for small to midsize businesses. They have built custom modules that do many of the things in the sales tech stack we're going to be discussing throughout this chapter. For small to midsize businesses, a tool like this that's easily customizable and quick to deploy might be a good all-in-one solution for those organizations that are typically sales and marketing driven and don't require a lot of custom or industry specific modules. The other big benefit of course is significantly less money per seat or user than a big tool like Salesforce or Microsoft Dynamics.

You want all the tools you choose, to play nicely and connect well with your CRM, which means if a tool like Gong.io or Shopify is important to your sales, marketing, and automation strategy then you are going to need to find a CRM that they integrate with. If you don't, then what occurs is that you'll find yourself as a sales leader and your sales team logging into multiple applications just to walk through the sales process and this is where most sales technology stacks fail to truly generate results. Every time a salesperson must switch tabs or log into a new system to do a sales task it disrupts their workflow, creates extra work, and creates the problem of having client data within multiple systems that don't talk to one another. So, for this reason, sometimes the least expensive CRM and sales tech tools can be the most expensive - the costs are more than just a monthly subscription, the costs are found in inefficiencies, inaccurate, or redundant data and not being able to truly execute a frictionless sales process. This disconnected stack is referred to as a Frankenstack and they often meet the same eventual fate that Frankenstein did after it wreaks havoc on your productivity. Poor sales technology that hinders the progress of sales performers will push them to seek work elsewhere – they will go work with someone who has a better tech stack. There are eight steps to choosing and implementing the right CRM solution for your organization:

1. **List which business processes and departments you want to improve with CRM use.**

   Your CRM selection should be entirely proactive and strategic, you need to develop your own criteria, business goals, and outcomes before beginning to shop around. The first aspect of this is to look at which departments in your organization you want your CRM to help integrate, systemize, and automate. Then carefully map out key steps and workflow that will be sequentially managed and/or automated. For your sales team, you should already have a solid sales process mapped out, benchmarked, and with all the core KPIs that you want to be measured and executed. As a sales performance specialist, one of the common challenges over the years that Shane Gibson has come across is the failure of CRM to actually improve a sales organization's performance. Many purchase the CRM, pay an organization to help them implement it, and then are surprised when nothing improves. The big reason is the CRM company generally isn't a sales process expertise company and they simply set up the CRM and map out what they think you might need or map out a process which you haven't yet perfected or truly proven. Without a good sales process, your CRM is not going to drive results.

2. **Seek out a CRM is capable of being aligned to your workflow through personalization.**

   After you have mapped out your core CRM processes and best practices, you should have a checklist and a visually mapped out sales and operational workflow that you want the CRM to drive. LucidChart is a great cloud-based business process mapping tool you can use to do this (and much more). You are now ready to shop around and start talking to various CRM companies and evaluating their solutions to see who can best help you automate and drive efficiencies in your sales marketing and other critical business processes. By getting this right you'll reduce the chance of your sales team members working outside of the CRM. If the CRM doesn't truly support best practices and help the salesperson, you'll find them working off spreadsheets, post-it notes, and unapproved third-party applications that actually help them execute their best practices. It's easier to find a CRM that will adapt to your teams' best practices then try to force your team to modify the way they work just so you can get some data into a CRM.

3. **Make sure that the CRM company or reseller can support you in a successful roll-out**

   Make sure your CRM company has a strong customer success process and team there to support you. Any new technology implementation in your organization is a change management exercise. A good CRM company or implementation partner will have a toolkit of best practices and processes that they have used to help organizations like yours successfully implement and launch. This should include training for staff on how to use the tool specifically for their function in the business. With any type of change, you're going to need to generate buy-in at multiple levels in your organization to make sure this implementation is successful, and a good CRM company will have a buy-in and education process mapped out to support you and your people. Many organizations are 100% remote or have remote staff so it's important that the training and implementation process is built to engage remote and virtual workers. This should include live as well as on-demand training modules, videos, and of course Technical Support.

4. **Ensure that the CRM is user-friendly and intuitive**

Make sure the CRM you choose is designed intuitively and is easy to navigate. If the interface is laid out ineffectively or looks outdated, you're already setting yourself up for an uphill battle for adoption. Some of the best CRM's have similar elements in similar places for a reason. It shouldn't have 22 different tabs to click on or need people to toggle between multiple screens just to complete a key task with the client. Your CRM should not visually look similar to a 747 dashboard, it should be as easy to navigate as Microsoft Word or Facebook. Another aspect of user friendliness is that the CRM must have an easy to use and fully functional mobile app that your team can use. A lot of sales executives spend time on their mobile phone calling clients or need to engage people while they're on the road. Having your CRM integrate with the smartphones of your team is a vital user-friendly function. If you don't have this there may be large parts of your team's day where they're executing core sales activities but can't easily enter data, record conversations, or be reminded of key steps they are supposed to execute.

5. **Pick a CRM that is an all-in-one sales tech stack or can integrate with leading tools**

Before choosing your CRM make sure you have a list of the core aspects of the sales tech stack that you need to either have integrated into a CRM already or can plug into it. Earlier we talked about ZOHO CRM and used it as an example of a CRM that is almost like a turnkey tech stack all in one. It includes many aspects such as marketing automation, email tracking, chat tools, and then of course contact management, email intelligence and automation, and numerous other tools. This may be a perfect solution for many organizations. You may want to look at a tool like Nimble CRM which is Jon Ferrara's latest award-winning CRM. This is a great choice if you are proactively using social selling and need to integrate with the Microsoft suite of Office solutions. Alternatively, if you are using Shopify as the primary channel to do business and then need your sales team to support that ecommerce enterprise through customer service and engagement then Shopify combined with a CRM like HubSpot might be your best choice. The point is for any unique business process there's likely an ideal combination of existing tools out there that can help you do it. The key is to make sure that you pick the CRM that either has the functionality you need or has the sales tech tools that you can plug into it from third parties seamlessly. No or very little computer programming should be required to do any of this.

6. **Ensure that reporting is easy and customizable**

Data and the interpretation of data are an incredibly important aspect of sales and marketing especially for those of us in leadership. if you have a well-integrated sales tech stack with your CRM and some good best practices implemented with your salespeople your data should be accurate and up to date. Integrity in our data is vital to helping us make the right business decisions and will help us to learn and iterate on that learning quickly. None of this is possible unless we can pull the right data out and present it in an easily understandable fashion. Make sure that the CRM you choose has a well built in and customizable reporting function where you can pull out the data you need visually, available daily or even in real-time. If this isn't a functionality within the CRM, then it must plug into and integrate with third party reporting tools that will help you as the leader get the data you need and make the right decisions. If someone in your organization has to spend days or hours collating spreadsheets every month or weekly it becomes a real waste of resources, and anyone who is actively worked with spreadsheets knows the chances of an error on every single spreadsheet that's given to you is high and once you collate all that data together there is a good chance that your numbers could be off. You cannot afford to fly blind or depend upon manual spreadsheets or no data whatsoever to make these business decisions. Find a good dashboard.

7. **Budget effectively for implementation**

A midsize sales organization that includes 30 sales professionals, five or six sales managers, a handful of customer service staff, and three to five senior executives, would total about $80,000 per year in licensing or monthly access costs for Salesforce. When you factor in migrating data from an old CRM, customizing the platform, plugging in 3rd party tools, and then training each team member as well as having a 90 day support plan in place to make sure the CRM is launched effectively your cost for that Salesforce implementation will actually be another $160,000 in additional implementation fees, consulting, integrations and training. The total cost in the first year is about $240,000 for a Salesforce implementation and software / Sales Cloud access. This cost of course will drop down to maybe $100,000 in the second year providing that you don't need any massive changes in process or updates and applications. This example includes all the bells and whistles, full customization, and consulting support. This may seem like a huge investment but if these 30 sales professionals each have a quota of $2,000,000 a year and we can increase their average deal size by 10% and the number of deals they land by 10% then the ROI of that CRM implementation can be quickly realized. You could calculate how much money they are losing by not having an effective CRM. Are they losing 2 or 3 100K deals each - every quarter?

Some CRMs start at about $20 US per user and after adding a few key functions might cost you $100 per sales professional per month, and many of these tools such as ZOHO or Nimble CRM have free online learning and self-directed tools to help your team implement. For 30 people this may cost you $36,000 a year for licensing plus another $10,000 for implementation costs and training. The reality is when you factor in your own internal teams' human capital costs, efforts and resources, and some moderate support externally it begins to add up. For every dollar you spend on the actual software license you will likely spend 1-5 more dollars in services implementation, customization, and data migration. This is the reality of a CRM implementation; it is vital to the success of your organization, but it is an investment. It's not a piece of capital equipment but you've got to look at it as a capital investment.

8. **Pick a tool that can support emerging and leading sales technologies and platforms**

There are vital emerging technologies that some CRM companies are beginning to implement, and others are still not even grasping the importance of it. There are some key CRM trends on the horizon that any leading CRM companies should have visibility to and are planning to integrate or build into their system. While there's not enough space in this book to talk about every emerging sales technology there are a few that are immediately becoming important tools and technologies that are giving the organizations that are using them a real advantage. If the CRM company you're talking to is not proactively using or about to implement these two technologies, you may want to look elsewhere. These technologies are AI or artificial intelligence and audio driven CRM.

Organizations like HubSpot and Salesforce have already built artificial intelligence modules into their CRM; it intelligently automates processes and even coaches salespeople on what their next step should be. Both of them published data recently that found that those sales professionals that were supported with an AI coach actually outperformed their peers win rates by over 20%. We will talk about artificial intelligence later on in this chapter and some of the AI based tools that you can plug into. Right now, for the purposes of this section on choosing a CRM, you need to make sure that the CRM company you're looking at either has AI or is implementing AI into their solution.

The other big trend which has already hit most of our households and our smartphones is voice commands and voice search as well as audio dictation. Tools like Google Home, Apple's Siri, or Amazon's Echo are all examples of voice technologies that make day-to-day activities and processes easier to execute, and in some cases, they can even auditorily coach or direct us when we need to take an action. We all know the one thing that salespeople hate the most is to waste time entering data into a CRM. The second thing they don't like to do is to try to find key pieces of information on clients or their contact details. They want both of these things to be seamless and easy and audio search, and audio commands are now being added to CRM and making it easier for your salespeople to enter and capture key talking points without having a huge impact on their daily productivity or proactive sales time.

Some tools (with the permission of staff and clients) can record entire conversations and then drop the transcript of that conversation into the notes section of the CRM, others go even further and begin to evaluate the quality of the conversation and key talking points that might need to be highlighted or actioned. This is where CRM is heading and where it becomes a true digital assistant to the sales professional instead of something that they have to put data into or record their activities in. The CRM of the future will drive activities and coach the sales professional truly making them more efficient and giving them more proactive selling time.

As we had mentioned earlier in the book, we are trying to stay away from giving you a shopping list of all the specific tech tools you want to look at. One of the reasons why is we could change our mind, or their technology could change, be replaced, or become completely obsolete in less than a year from now. With that said, CRM has been around since 1989 and will continue to be around in some form for many years to come, for that reason we'd like to provide you with a list of CRMs that have either stood the test of time or have a good potential chance of being the next market leader. This list should give you a good starting point of CRMs that you should look into, these organizations are as follows:

- Microsoft Dynamics
- Salesforce
- Nimble
- ZOHO
- HubSpot
- Pipelinedeals
- Maximizer
- Sugar CRM
- SAP CRM
- Oracle on Demand CRM

LEAD GENERATION AND PROSPECTING

Lead generation and prospecting are the core top of the funnel function that many sales organizations spend a lot of time and energy focusing on. Prospecting for new business proactively is one of the best ways you can ensure that you're attracting the right type of clients. There is a whole industry that has evolved in the tech space that is specifically focused on developing and providing tools to help make sales professionals and sales organizations better at generating leads and prospecting for new accounts.

Some tools will observe existing customer behavior on your website and then notify your sales team that that particular person has downloaded a new white paper or filled out a shopping cart and then abandon it. These types of prospecting tools help qualify or prioritize who your team might want to reach out to. HubSpot CRM for instance has a module built into it that integrates with your website that does just that.

Other tools like Outreach.io allow you to build custom workflows or sequences for each type of prospect and then they either automate or semi automate the whole process for your team. Based upon best of breed business practices or your own unique process Outreach can help you execute a series of social media, email, and voice driven interactions that help you take a prospect from being a suspect to being a qualified and closed client.

Although it would fall under the category of a social selling tool LinkedIn Sales Navigator has some strong lead generation and prospecting functionality built into it as well. A lot of prospecting is about reaching out in the right context and with the right timing with key prospects. By understanding your ideal client profile and then tracking key ideal clients and prospects, Sales Navigator can let you know of major events or changes in your prospect behavior that indicate an opportunity to begin a conversation or reach out to them.

Following are a list of leading and innovative prospecting and lead generation tools or CRMs that include this functionality in them:

- Outreach.io
- LinkedIn Sales Navigator
- HubSpot
- Shapr
- Drift
- Prospect.io
- Leadfeeder
- Bombora

By investing in one or more of these prospecting and lead development tools you are automating or building efficiencies into the quality and velocity of ideal leads that your team can generate. Many of these tools save hours per week per rep by reducing manual activities, research, and minimizing the number of bad decisions around where to invest time and with whom.

CONTACT ENRICHMENT AND INTELLIGENCE

Contact enrichment and intelligence tools are invaluable. These are typically large intelligently organized databases of millions of contacts that you have access to on a pay per use basis. When your sales team is reaching out to a potential prospect, they may start off with a LinkedIn profile and if they're lucky with an email address, sometimes they just have the first and last name and a company name. Seldomly do companies list the direct phone numbers or emails of senior executives on their website, these are often coveted and hard to find pieces of data.

Contact enrichment tools will often have these types of private contact information available on a per contact pricing basis. You can get a lot of background information on the individual, corporate insights, regional insights, and even lists of social media profiles and other supplementary sources of information that can help you. It's possible for a person to dig this information up on their own but it takes many minutes if not hours to put together a shortlist of people and their key contact information and research.

Contact enrichment and intelligence tools can get you all this information with the click of a button and save you hours per day as a proactive prospector. If you multiply this across 10, 20, or 30 sales professionals in an organization digging up contact intelligence can be expensive. In addition to this anytime someone is spending time researching they're not selling or communicating to customers and prospects, if too much time is spent doing this it often reduces job satisfaction for the sales professional. These tools can either directly be accessed through your CRM or can be easily imported.

Following is a list of contact enrichment and intelligence tools:

- Insideview
- Datanyze
- Zoominfo
- Nimble CRM (feature within the CRM)
- D&B Hoovers
- LinkedIn Sales Navigator (limited data points)
- Crunchbase
- ClearBit

E-MAIL INTELLIGENCE AND AUTOMATION TOOLS

Email intelligence and automation tools are important parts of a sales professional's toolkit. One of the key functionalities of these email intelligence tools is to track your emails and let you know when they are opened, if the attachments are opened up, and what links are clicked on within the emails. Nimble CRM has this built directly into their email program and has integrated with Microsoft Outlook and GMAIL. HubSpot Sales has much of the same functionality with some additional tracking where you even get to know what region the person is geographically located in when they open your email.

This can be quite an important sales tool especially if you sent a proposal to someone and then they've gone dark or haven't answered in a while. Three or four weeks later you get a notification they've opened your email and clicked on your proposal. Right at that moment you could pick up the phone and call them and say something like, "Hey I've been thinking about you and I thought I'd just reach out and follow up on our conversation we had last month." Being able to reach out and talk to a potential customer within a reasonable timeframe of when they are thinking specifically about your solution increases the chance that they're going to be receptive to you and that your call will be on topic. These tools can be used to measure the email and follow up success rates of team members across your company. It allows you to dig deeper and discover why specific people have better open rates or get more proposals read and then share that information with the rest of the team.

Automation functionality within your email system is important. Some of your emails need to be highly customized and contextualized based upon the stage of the sales cycle or what the customers told you they need. Many emails however require minimal customization just a change in someone's name, company name, and possibly a specific reference to a product they purchased in the past. All of these things can be pulled out of your CRM in an automated fashion and allow you to send an email to a segment of your customers without having to cut and paste and manually customize each email for dozens or hundreds of people. This allows you to scale a customized outreach to a specific segment and then utilizing the tracking features to know who's opened your email, what links they've clicked on, or if they've downloaded your most recent brochure or thought leadership piece. You have to be careful to not over- automate but it's important to scale parts of your prospecting, account based marketing, and lead nurturing through automation where appropriate.

Following is a selection of some of the popular email intelligence and automation tools available out there, it's important to notice in this list that several CRM's are listed as well because their systems come with this functionality:

- HubSpot Sales
- YesWare
- Outreach.io
- Mailtrack.io
- Nimble CRM
- ZOHO CRM
- Prospect.io
- Boomerang

SALES WORKFLOW

Sales workflow tools help take your sales process with all of its incremental steps and contact points and organize them for you. It's important to note that the steps that may be required over time to close a mid-level deal are going to be quite different than those that are required to upsell an existing client or close a large enterprise client.

This means an individual salesperson may have half a dozen or more different types of cadences and follow up processes for different client segments and for different relationship stages. Each of these cadences will have their own unique talking points, sales enablement content, and discovery meeting questions. This is a lot of variation and a lot of different best practices that would have to be taught to a sales professional. Left to their own devices it's unlikely that they're going to be able to replicate the best practices you want them to on a consistent basis.

A sales workflow system like Salesloft allows you to map out each step of your customer follow up or nurturing process, and at each of these steps connect it to sales enablement content such as scripts or talking points, thought leadership content to be sent, or even a full needs analysis or discovery question agenda that they can follow.

Essentially a good sales workflow tool will tell you when it's time to execute a specific step and then give you content and best practices to execute that step effectively.

A person can easily profile a prospect, sign them to a specific category, and then your sales workflow tool will launch the appropriate cadence or lead nurturing process for the sales team member. Some aspects of this process can be fully automated, while others are just reminders to reach out manually and engage the prospective customer. The biggest benefit to this is that it helps your sales team execute a proven process for converting and engaging prospects. The other benefit is in onboarding training and launching new sales team members. If you're using a good sales workflow tool your new sales team members can start selling and have direct guidance in a successful sales process much quicker than those that don't have a sales workflow system that is coaching them and prompting them through each step of the sales process.

Following is a short list of some of the leading sales workflow tools or CRM with sales workflow functionality built in them:

- Salesloft
- Engagio
- ZOHO CRM
- MEMBRAIN (For complex and enterprise sales)
- HubSpot
- Prospect.io
- Autoklose
- Velocify

COMMUNICATIONS AND ENGAGEMENT

The communications and engagement category of sales tech tools encompasses all the tools and technologies that your sales team could leverage to have one to one or one to many communications with their client's prospects and the community at large. Digital communications and engagement tools are vital if we're going to compete and sell in the virtual economy. These aren't just digital tools but any tool that is utilized to sell from a remote perspective. It's important to think about what channels of communication your existing or potential customers are going to want to engage your sales team on. It's important to think about what tools are going to help your sales team stand out or cut through the noise. Following are three key categories of engagement tools you may want to invest in:

1) Multi-media messaging

   One example of an innovative engagement tool that you may want to look at utilizing for your team is something like Vidyard or Loom. Both tools allow you to record and send short video messages to clients and prospects. Each video tracks the engagement, number of views, and shares. Links in these videos can be included in the body of an email, a LinkedIn or Twitter private message, or posted directly to a social network publicly. The emails and landing pages for these videos can be branded and customized. This of course is just one example of a digital engagement tool.

2) Web meeting and webinar tools

Another category of communications and engagement tools are of course video meeting platforms and webinar tools. Although we haven't had a chance to address this, training your team in effective web video meeting formats, technologies, and best practices is vital to your success as a remote and virtual selling organization. Choosing a tool that works for you and your clients is vital. Zoom video is the mass market tool of choice, others include WebEx, GoToMeeting, Microsoft Teams, and dozens of other secure and professional web meeting, and video communications tools.

The key is to select the right tool and then train your team on both the technical aspects but equip them with best practices and training on how to conduct great video meetings. Another aspect of this is selecting the right webinar platform. You may find that Microsoft Teams works well for you to conduct small group meetings, but if your sales team is responsible for conducting webinars and engaging groups of prospects you may want to look at investing in a Zoom Webinar license or something like GotoWebinar as an additional tool that this designed specifically for large group engagement.

> *Another aspect to setting your sales team up for success utilizing web meetings and webinar tools is investing in the hardware and production tools needed for them to look professional.*

Another aspect to setting your sales team up for success utilizing web meetings and webinar tools is investing in the hardware and production tools needed for them to look professional. These include but are not limited to:

- *A professional background for video meetings*
- *An HD quality web camera*
- *A professional microphone or high-quality headset*
- *Proper lighting/lights*
- *An additional monitor to help them manage and coordinate the video meeting*
- *Professional training and coaching on conducting great video meetings*

3) Chat tools and instant messaging tools

Chat software like Drift, Facebook Messenger, or ones that are built right into our CRM like ZOHO's chat feature could be found in many parts of the sales stack, but we decided to put it here. Chat can obviously be the first line of communication with the prospect, but it could be the preferred line of communication for an existing customer. Tools like WhatsApp would also fall under this category. Being able to reach out and send a quick question to your account manager can be of high value to a busy executive. It gives a sales professional an advantage if they can have this type of channel of communication open and accessible to their key accounts and prospects. ZOHO has a feature where if you click on a link in a sales executive's signature it may take you directly to their corporate website but the chat box that pops up will directly connect the person to that sales executive's mobile phone where they can chat via text.

Following is a list of the tools we discussed in this section and a few additional notable ones you may want to look at:

- Vidyard
- Loom
- Zoom Meetings
- Zoom Webinar
- WebEx
- GoToMeeting
- GotoWebinar
- Microsoft Teams
- Skype Video
- Drift
- Facebook Messenger
- WhatsApp

SOCIAL SELLING

There are a few key social selling tools that you need to add to your sales tech stack. The categories we will discuss are social media management software, content development apps and platforms, relevant mobile apps from each social network, social selling, and sales team advocacy tools.

Social media management software like Hootsuite, Socxo, and to some degree Sprout Social can help individuals and sales teams manage their content, track hashtags, schedule posts on multiple networks, and track the click-throughs and engagement of their content and shares. Being able to build a content calendar and then plug key posts and social content into them over a week or a one-month period can help social sellers become expert curators and thought leaders.

Sales teams can use tools like PostBeyond and Oktopost to share company sales enablement content in an organized fashion and create a single access point for current content that's easy to share. LinkedIn has now built this type of functionality directly into LinkedIn business pages allowing businesses to notify key staff when they post new content to their page so that their team can then share that content in a timely fashion.

Depending on the brand and what social network you and your sales team have decided to focus on it's important that the individual sales team members add the relevant mobile apps for each social network to their smartphones. Instagram for instance only works on a mobile phone or tablet if you want to publish to your network, and LinkedIn has specific functionality on the mobile app that doesn't actually exist in the desktop application. Tools like Hootsuite and Sprout Social have their own mobile apps.

Video and other types of content creation are vital to success in social selling and social media marketing so it's important we have the tools we need to effectively create content on the fly. Canva.com is a great example of a user-friendly platform loaded with millions of images and videos that are ready to be edited, branded, and then published to various channels that you are active on. A creative salesperson with a little bit of training and a few brand guidelines is able to create images, videos, and even infographics that they can share with their networks or use in their one-to-one communications with key prospects. Depending upon the amount of publishing the sales pros or sales team is doing you may want to look at a membership to a site like Shutterstock or Unsplash where you can buy access to royalty free images to use in your social media posts.

LinkedIn's Sales Navigator is a paid subscription and social selling tool that is built right into LinkedIn's platform. Sales Navigator is probably the most important social sales app for anyone wanting to leverage that social network for business. CRM's like Microsoft Dynamics and Sugar CRM and tools like Outreach.io have direct integrations with Sales Navigator.

As a bare minimum the social sellers on your sales team should have a social media management tool to help them schedule and publish content, key content development apps and platforms to keep their posts looking professional and engaging, as well as social network mobile apps and a membership to LinkedIn Sales Navigator.

Following is a short list of key social selling tools apps and networks that you may want to look at investing in for your team:

- Hootsuite
- Socxo
- Sprout Social
- PostBeyond
- Oktopost
- Instagram Business account + app
- LinkedIn Sales Navigator
- Outreach.io
- Buzz Sumo
- Canva.com
- Shutterstock
- Unsplash

CLOSING

There are specific apps and tools that can help sales professionals seal the deal while selling remotely. PandaDoc and DocuSign allow you to digitally sign and track key documents to maintain security but remotely they help get deals closed. Proposify is another great closing tool. Many times, proposals can take so much time to prepare that by the time we get it to the client they've cooled off. Proposify helps you build an online library of winning proposals and templates them in a way that allows your team to quickly generate custom proposals and get them sent directly to the client. This tool of course allows electronic signatures and has functionality built into generate contracts as well.

Without these types of tools, it's difficult to have a fully remote sales process. The last thing you want to do is slow down a deal because you're waiting for a contract to be couriered and signed in hardcopy.

Leading and innovative digital closing tools to consider include:

- Adobe Acrobat Pro DC
- PandaDoc
- DocuSign
- SignNow
- HelloSign
- Proposify
- Qwilr
- Formstack

ARTIFICIAL INTELLIGENCE

AI and machine learning are now so prevalent across all aspects of the tech stack that we debated even including this as a separate aspect of the tech stack. Many of the tools we've already talked about actually have some sort of artificial intelligence built in. With that said we thought we would highlight some of the types of artificial intelligence that are available as both standalone tools and integrations. Your goal with artificial intelligence is to help your team automate repetitive tasks, improve decision making through actionable insights, and ultimately still create an engaging and enchanting experience for the end user or customer.

Tools like Conversica take the concept of sales workflow and engagement to the next level. Using a library of questions and answers with the ability to interpret customer responses and intent it will engage a customer or potential customer through chat or email with a series of back and forth communications to help grade that potential opportunity. It can even book that person into the calendar of a sales executive. Tools like this can increase the speed of engagement and response times with potential and existing clients while escalating the best opportunities to a live agent.

Crystal Knows another one of our favorites and is an AI driven personality profile reader. It analyzes email communications and the online social footprint and posts of anyone you select and then using the DISC™ personality assessment model it determines what the individual's personality and communications preferences are (based upon the data). It includes a library of templates for emails, including what you might want to say to a particular personality style when booking an appointment, following up on the proposal, cold prospecting, and a myriad of other business communications topics. Although it is only moderately accurate in comparison to in depth personality profile tools, it's a great starting point and definitely helps move sales reps away from a one size fits all communication strategy.

Gong.io is an industry leading and powerfully disruptive AI based tool that can significantly help improve how you and your team communicate. Their platform listens to your sales team's phone conversations, and web meetings then transcribes them and evaluates speech patterns, keywords used, price discussions, and even matching and mirroring of tone, pace, and cadence of the communication. Based upon a massive data set of winning sales conversations Gong then presents the sales leader with a dashboard profiling which sales team members are having productive conversations that are likely to lead to a close and those that might be talking too much, or talking too early about things like price or mentioning competitors names too often. Sales organizations that have implemented this artificial intelligence-based tool have had significant gains in win rates, as well as net increases in the size of the average deal their team is closing.

Other AI based assistants can automatically book meetings for you into your calendar while acting like a virtual personal assistant communicating back and forth with your clients via email or chatbots. On the topic of chatbots, these AI based tools are great for prequalifying and engaging online leads and customers. Chatbots can escalate conversations to a live agent once the conversation gets too complex or the customer or prospect triggers a series of criteria that make it a high-quality lead or potential conversion.

This topic of AI and the future of sales is actually so important that it's worthy of an entire book but for the purposes of this book, we wanted to introduce the power of AI to you and urge you to research how you can deploy it strategically to give you and your team the competitive advantage in the marketplace. A list of potential AI driven tools that you could leverage include:

- Salesforce Einstein
- HubSpot
- Grammarly
- Conversica
- X.ai
- Crystal Knows
- Gong.io
- Nudge
- People.ai
- Chorus.ai

In the following pages, there are two worksheets designed to help you build your sales technology stack. The first worksheet will help you organize your process for selecting a CRM. The second worksheet will help you plan your Sales Technology Stack.

In the below CRM Vendor Worksheet list your top 3 choices for your CRM. Next, evaluate and make notes on how each CRM performs in each category. Summarize your reasoning for picking the "winner" in the final section at the bottom of the Worksheet.

CRM Vendor Worksheet			
List your top 3 pics for CRM evaluation:	Vendor 1:	Vendor 2:	Vendor 3:
Aligned or customizable to our unique and vital processes?			
Has a support system for successful roll-out and implementation?			
User friendly and intuitive CRM interface and functions?			
All-in-one sales stack or integrates with key sales tech tools needed?			
Easy and customizable reporting and dashboards?			
Within our allotted budget?			
Supports emerging and leading sales technologies?			
Assists in coaching and guiding reps through sales best practices?			
Cloud based / SaaS (Software as a service)?			
Other:			
Chosen CRM solution and summarized business case or reasoning for purchase:			

Use this worksheet to map-out the key components of your sales technology stack. Select the Sales Technology Stack components that you would like to add to your stack, then list which software or tool vendor you will be using, and in the third column talk about your expected sales process improvements or expected ROI from implementing the tool. Under other, you can list additional sales technology stack components that might be needed for your industry.

Sales Technology Stack Worksheet		
Sales Technology Stack Component	Which Software, App(s), or Platform(s)?	Expected improvements or ROI?
CRM		
Lead Generation and Prospecting		
Contact Enrichment and Intelligence		
E-mail intelligence and Automation Tools		
Sales Workflow		
Communications and Engagement		
Social Selling		
Closing		
Artificial Intelligence		
Other:		
Other:		
Other:		

In the writing of the next two chapters, we asked Julian Lee to contribute his wisdom and 30+ years of experience in the technology space. He has worked almost every major technology vendor on the planet helping them develop their partnership channels.

CHAPTER 9

THE WEAKEST LINK IN YOUR DIGITAL GAME

"Computer security, cybersecurity or information technology security is the protection of computer systems and networks from the theft of or damage to their hardware, software, or electronic data, as well as from the disruption or misdirection of the services they provide."

WIKIPEDIA.

The media has covered many recent massive cyber-attacks and data breaches that have cost businesses millions and eroded client confidence given that their sensitive personal files have been compromised. Hackers typically access names, social security numbers, birth dates, addresses, medical and driver's license information, as well as credit card numbers, essentially all the critical data required for identity theft. It is estimated that 80% of consumers will defect from a business if their information is compromised in a breach.

Many small and medium sized businesses are under the illusion that cybercriminals only target large corporations, government, and financial institutions. The fact is that 58% of cyber-attack victims are small businesses, unfortunately, because they mistakenly think they are not being targeted they normally don't have cybersecurity front of mind.

Once you go digital, protecting your data is no longer an option. This represents more profits than all of the global trade of illegal drugs combined.

- JULIAN LEE

"The annual cost of global cybercrime in 2021 is predicted to be $6 trillion" Cybersecurity Ventures.

Deputy Attorney General Rod J. Rosenstein on cyber-attacks, "If you think it won't happen to your company, you are probably wrong. A private report put the risk of suffering a material data breach at better than one in four — and the odds continue to rise… Private reports peg the average cost of a data breach at over $3.6 million. But of course, that is an average. One large retailer reported spending $291 million for breach-related expenses, related to one attack on its network. In some cases, smaller businesses declare bankruptcy after a breach. Even if your company does not hold large quantities of financial information, it almost certainly has valuable intellectual property in its computer systems.

Ransomware is now a global phenomenon. The FBI estimates that ransomware infected more than 100,000 computers a day around the world. That number continues to grow. The total amount of ransom payments approaches $1 billion annually. Attacks used to be indiscriminate, scattershot attempts to squeeze a few hundred dollars from anyone who happened to be affected. Today, we see more sophisticated and targeted attacks that focus on particular businesses or sectors."

Costs resulting from cybercrimes include money, downtime for the business, theft of intellectual property, data loss, personal information and reputation. When a company's data is attacked or stolen, the ramifications can be so massive that it can bankrupt a business.

Even consumers can get their data encrypted or locked up by hackers and have to pay a ransom to retrieve. Imagine losing all of your family photos or other important documents. What would you pay to get them back?

Most industry experts, government officials, universities, cybersecurity companies, and experts have all expressed the same concerns about the cybersecurity threats facing businesses, governments. and consumers. News media outlets are constantly reporting the latest mega attacks but those are only a tiny fraction of the overall volume. No one is immune to ransomware attacks.

Cybercriminals can be individuals, organized gangs, or governments. The prize can be money or business intelligence. Political and election interference is on the rise.

Attack vectors by cybercriminals are expanding to include IoT devices, wearable devices, and even the security companies who are protecting their customers. Working remotely is becoming a new normal and that means there are now more attack vectors than ever before into businesses. Every device with an IP address in the home can be an entry point of attack through the remote user.

Data volumes are growing by leaps and bounds every day. Microsoft estimates that data volumes will be 50 times greater by the end of 2020 than they were in 2016. IoT devices are growing into the hundreds of billions. All this means that the attack surface is getting bigger year over year.

Protecting the data is mission critical for any business and there are many moving parts to doing this right. Hackers only need to find one vulnerability. You have to think of protecting every possibility. It is a cat and mouse game and so far, the hackers are ahead.

Hacking can include more than just business networks and computers. It can include heart pacemakers, automobiles, and medical devices. Trillions of sensors are embedded in devices everywhere and all of them are potential attack entry points for hackers.

Typically, there are about 8 layers of cybersecurity protection that leading companies deploy. Most companies do not have such a sophisticated approach or a large budget to protect their data. That said, every business must continually reduce the level of vulnerability to attacks as much as possible.

We will not go through the various layers of protection but give you a sense of how you need to think about protecting your business from hackers. You will need professional cybersecurity experts or organizations to help you build out your protection, monitoring, and mediation.

When sophisticated hackers breach a system, they just keep quiet and watch and wait from the optimal moment to launch their attack. Sometimes they just monitor activities to learn secrets. Sometimes they slowly extract your data and threaten to release it publicly if you do not pay a ransom.

As such, it is wise to include a "hunt" program to uncover potential malware and vulnerable points on your network. Penetration testing (PEN) is a smart way to probe your network and systems to identify potential weaknesses so you can fix them before hackers do.

Hopefully, this information so far has opened your eyes as to the scope of the problem that cyber-attacks can cause your business and give you some good reasons for making it a top priority in your plans.

So now what?

JULIAN LEE'S 15 RULES FOR CYBER PROTECTION

After interviewing hundreds of cybersecurity experts, I have compiled a short list of their best recommendations to protect your business from cyber-attacks. By no means is this an all-encompassing list, but if you can nail these items down, you are definitely moving in the right direction.

1. One of the smartest things a business can do is to educate their workforce about the dangers of cyber threats and how everyone has a duty and responsibility to reduce the risk. There should be a cybersecurity policy in place regarding spam mail, public WIFI usage, downloading files, website visits, and overall online behaviors.

2. Penetration Testing (PEN) to find potential vulnerabilities in your network can be a great starting point. This is when a "good" hacker is hired to try to break into your network to identify your weak spots in your security. You will know one way or another just how secure you are. There are several tools that can help you to do sophisticated assessments quickly and more cost-effectively.

3. Cybersecurity Awareness Training is a must for all of your employees so they understand how hackers could target them and how to recognize the basics to more advanced attacks. The vast majority of hacks happen through "phishing". This tricks a user into clicking on a link delivered by email which in turn,

downloads malware to the device and network. With solid employee training, most of these cyber-attacks can be prevented.

4. Protecting the wireless network perimeter with multiple layers of security applications and firewall devices. This includes your entire network infrastructure and all endpoints (computers, smartphones, tablets, servers, routers, etc.) that connect to it. This requires well trained professionals to configure, install and maintain firewalls, anti-virus, and other preventative and detection solutions to protect and mediate.

5. Password management. The easiest way to access any network is through a stolen password. Hackers have tools that can easily "guess" simple passwords.

   Keep passwords complex and secure at all times. This is challenging and frustrating for most people as they typically have to remember many passwords and logins. There are several applications and devices currently available that can help you manage your passwords securely while making it easier for the user. You hear a lot about "2-factor authentication" because it is a simple and good layer of protection from password hacking (basically when the system is accessed with your credentials, it will send a confirmation request with a PIN number to your phone that you must enter to continue your access).

6. Remote working. Whenever the user is outside of the secured network or perimeter, they become vulnerable to attacks. Accessing public WIFI or logging into your network from devices that are unsecured can be an easy way for hackers to penetrate your system. Locking down wireless access and using solutions like VPNs can reduce the risks, but you need to balance performance and productivity.

7. Assess your security provider. Do you do due diligence on whomever you hire to protect your business from cyber-attacks? Verify that they are fully qualified to do the job right. This is one area that you cannot afford to make a mistake because of their incompetence. You want to ensure that they are protecting themselves as they are a common attack vector by hackers (break into them and get access to all their clients). There are independent organizations that assess and certify security providers to help guide you.

8. A backup and disaster recovery plan is mission critical for any business against attacks. Since no one can offer any guarantees that you will never be breached, you need a plan B. That is to have your data backed up offsite and to multiple locations so you can retrieve it if all else fails. Ensure that your backup solution can protect from malware being embedded in your backups as that can severely damage your backup data and your time to recovery. Test your backup and recovery to ensure it works! Note, cost, and time to recover from a backup can be shocking so get some insights into this before you have no choice.

9. Sensible user defined policies. Several solutions are now available to help set various policies and limits for every user to ensure each only has access to what they need. This is important because data breaches can be from within by employees (knowingly or unknowingly). Security solutions can automatically

monitor network traffic for anything that seems out of the normal so they can intervene and block in real-time, if necessary.

10. Real time monitoring and mediation. You do not want to leave your protection to just the technology and AI is still in the early days to take over the task. You need humans to monitor the activities and intervene in real time to prevent attacks as they happen. This can dramatically reduce the potential damage. Security Operations Centres (SOC) are organizations to consider because they are dedicated to offering the highest levels of cyber protection with 24/7 monitoring and mediation.

11. Use web and e-mail filters. This will help you to reduce the amount of spam and other potentially more harmful phishing emails from getting to your employee's devices. It will block malware from being downloaded when browsing websites.

12. Donate or dispose of old computers and media carefully. Ensure data is wiped clean and in a way that is not recoverable. Many companies offer this service to shred your data media.

13. Patching software. Every business uses a variety of software applications. When vendors add functionality or discover security vulnerabilities, they send updates. If you do not download and execute the update, then your application is left exposed to an attack. Constant patching of apps and operating systems is an easy effective way to dramatically and instantly improve the level of your security.

14. Compliance. In some regions and countries, the law requires you to protect your customers' data. Governmental compliance laws and protecting your customer information and privacy is a growing issue. Failure to protect your customer information or disclose breaches in a timely manner can result in hefty fines and other more severe legal consequences plus damage to your reputation. Your insurance coverage may be impacted by your level of security protection.

15. Forensics investigation after an attack. In the likely event that despite all of your best efforts, you may still get hacked. If that happens, you will need to do a comprehensive investigation to figure out what happened, how, when, why, and where. This will allow you to improve your security for the future and may help authorities to press the hackers.

16. Remember that cybersecurity is a moving target that can morph into something unexpected in an instant. The ability to anticipate what is not expected and prevent an attack from ever happening is the end game. It is a constant learning experience and battle to stop the next attack.

You will hear a lot about Artificial Intelligence being used by companies to help prevent cyber-attacks but remember that hackers can also use AI. Many vendors are already integrating some level of AI into their technology and the impact is significant. AI will continue to play an increasingly important role in the prevention of cyber-attacks.

The latest buzzword in security is called "Zero Trust". Zero Trust may be a wise approach to the best secret practices. PaltoAlto networks summed it up best...

"Zero Trust is a strategic initiative that helps prevent successful data breaches by eliminating the concept of trust from an organization's network architecture. Rooted in the principle of "never trust, always verify," Zero Trust is designed to protect modern digital environments by leveraging network segmentation, preventing lateral movement, providing Layer 7 threat prevention, and simplifying granular user-access control.

Zero Trust was created by John Kindervag, during his tenure as a vice president and principal analyst for Forrester Research, based on the realization that traditional security models operate on the outdated assumption that everything inside an organization's network should be trusted. Under this broken trust model, it is assumed that a user's identity is not compromised and that all users act responsibly and can be trusted. The Zero Trust model recognizes that trust is a vulnerability. Once on the network, users – including threat actors and malicious insiders – are free to move laterally and access or exfiltrate whatever data they are not limited to. Remember, the point of infiltration of an attack is often not the target location."

As businesses accelerate into digital transformation, they will be putting more online access to their data, systems, and people. That will increase their risks of being hacked. Banks put the cash in a vault to stop robbers and employees from getting easy access. Banks would not leave the vault's door open or not have adequate security protection measures in place. Think of cybersecurity in the same way. How thick and secure do you need to make your "vault door" and its perimeter to protect your data?

Navigating your needs for cyber-attack prevention can be a daunting task. Business managers are simply ill-equipped to properly understand the full scope of something as complex as cybersecurity. Finding the right cybersecurity provider in your local region can also be a challenge but it is a critical requirement for reducing your risks.

In the next chapter, we will outline what you should be looking for as you interview for the right solutions provider to do the job.

CHAPTER 10

READY TO START YOUR DIGITAL TRANSFORMATION JOURNEY?

Remember that digital transformation (DT) is all about outcomes. You will need a solid digital transformation strategy and a qualified team to achieve the desired outcomes. This will ultimately reshape your business into one that leverages a variety of technologies to improve operations on every level and deliver better outcomes to your customers, employees. and shareholders.

This will take a pragmatic approach to deliver measured incremental changes to eventually become a fully digital business. It's a long journey that will deliver improved outcomes along the way. It takes time!

Start by looking for some quick wins to kick off the journey. There are always parts of a business that needs a lift, so maybe start there. There are several Robotic Processing Automation (RPA) and Business Process Automation (BPA) solutions that allow companies to quickly and easily build custom applications to solve significant problems. It's easy enough to do some of this development in- house and cost-effectively.

RPA and BPA solutions may be one way to generate some quick wins in the beginning phase of your DT journey. Keep on looking for more "ready-made" solutions and partners with the right skills to show positive outcomes.

However, a comprehensive digital transformation has many layers of complexity and requires specialized knowledge and skills to deliver. Most companies simply do not have this pool of talent in-house. It is highly unlikely that just one company could provide everything you need. As such, you will need to hire several partners to build the required ecosystem of talent to successfully deliver on your digital transformation journey and outcomes.

One of the biggest challenges you will have is sorting through the smoke and mirrors to identify the right talent and expertise.

First, be careful of people who layer a digital talk over their traditional systems and thinking. Many can talk the talk but not all can walk the walk. A good story is not what you need. You will need to do your proper research and due diligence upfront or your journey may be a very long and winding road or worst, you may get lost.

Before you start outsourcing, you should first look at your internal strengths and weaknesses. Make a plan to identify and find the available internal talent and skills that could be leveraged for DT. You may be surprised to learn just how much expertise you already have within your organization. You should consider offering some additional training to your internal team to get the required digital skills.

Having internal champions is important for ensuring a smooth and effective digital adoption and transformation. This in-house effort could increase the level of internal support to actually speed up the overall success of the transformation while improving employee morale. Going through this first exercise to better understand your internal strengths will make it easier to figure out what you need to outsource and could save costs.

Doing a Google search to find what you need is probably not going to be enough. You will find an avalanche of information and ads pitching all sorts of angles and components for digital transformation. You can certainly learn a lot by digesting all of this content, but it can be confusing and misleading.

The end goal is to find, evaluate, and select the right mix of tools and services that best meet your needs. Keep in mind that all of the pieces of the puzzle have to work well together from an integration and security perspective. Sometimes you may need to forgo the better solution for the solution that is better integrated with what you have. It is about compromise, but not to a point where it jeopardizes your business outcomes.

Your selected partner(s) will first need to carefully review all of your requirements and build out the most appropriate solutions and IT infrastructure to meet those needs. This professional upfront consultative work is necessary. You may even want to have several independent DT consultants provide their assessment and roadmap to compare and verify. Be cautious of vendor brand sales pitches for the obvious reason that they could be biased.

The partner(s) that you choose will be tasked to acquire the DT technologies, customize, and implement. They will have to train your staff on how to use and manage. They will need to monitor and maintain the entire digital ecosystem 365 days a year to ensure it is always performing well. There are several components to consider when choosing your partners and everything should have seamless continuity.

Keep in mind that for every $1 you spend on a license for an application, you could expect to spend between $4 and $9 for customization, implementation, and maintenance. Unless you can and are prepared to do the work yourself, there are no shortcuts. Some partners may discount prices but be careful that they will be still able to deliver on time and on expectations. Cheaper rates are relative to the time spent doing the job. You should always calculate the total cost of ownership vis-a-vis outcomes when comparing partner quotes and agreements.

The most common outsourced partner is typically called a "Managed Services Provider" (MSP) or an Information Technology Solution Provider (ITSP), Independent

Software Vendor (ISV), Managed Security Service Provider (MSSP) or Security Operations Centre (SOC) and sometimes a Value-Added Reseller (VAR). That said, they do come in all shapes and sizes. The MSP type of companies is most common in the partner ecosystem as they specialize in providing complex and comprehensive multi-vendor IT solutions for digital transformation with continuous monitoring and maintenance. Their fees are typically based on a monthly pay-as-you-go plan.

Implementing the right DT infrastructure requires an ongoing collaborative effort by talented professionals as well as experts from third-parties, ISVs, and key vendors who have developed the DT platforms and related technologies.

Your selected partner will be responsible for maintaining and predicting your future IT needs as they continue to improve your operations and reduce your capital expenses. It will be a long-term partnership.

Clients and partners are bound by a Service Level Agreement (SLA). It's a legal document that basically outlines all of the details on how all services will be monitored and managed to ensure maximum uptime. The cost will vary depending on the type and how fast you need support turnaround to be so you will need to decide on your requirements for the SLA. Keep in mind that some partners may physically not be able to deliver on all of your SLA requirements so you will have to negotiate this upfront to set expectations on both sides. If your business needs 100% uptime within 60 minutes, then you need to ensure that your selected partner can do that.

Partners will usually provide periodic reports to the client to outline what has been happening in comparison to the SLA. You want regular reporting to ensure you are getting exactly what you are paying for or so you can adjust as your needs change.

Partners should be able to combine most of the customer's IT requirements and services for one predictable monthly fee that is usually based per user or per device. This fee will range depending on what solutions are implemented, software licensing requirements/costs, and the level of managed services are required.

As the partner gets to better understand your business, they should be able to recommend more solutions and services that will continually improve your business productivity and reduce costs. You should think of a digital transformation partner as an organization that will empower your business with the best technologies and processes while constantly finding new ways to reduce costs and improve outcomes.

Digital transformation is not only about applications or security or devices or platforms. You need to take into consideration access by your employees and customers. Performance matters. What happens if you get a DDoS attack that knocks out your access. Accessibility, performance, and security are all equally important. All technologies will need to be implemented and orchestrated to ensure optimal performance, access, and security.

So, how do you find a digital transformation partner that is right for you?

Not all partners are created equal. Unfortunately, most do sound alike and use similar content on their websites and marketing tools. When all of the "book covers" look the same, it becomes difficult to know what makes each different or who is ultimately the right fit for you.

THERE ARE 5 BASIC ELEMENTS THAT YOU WANT TO LOOK FOR IN A DIGITAL TRANSFORMATION PARTNER:

1. **Industry Specific Experience**. Look for partners with solid experience in your industry as they are most likely to know what you need and have the required skills and tools to deliver. Benefit from their experience of helping similar companies in your industry.

2. **Strong Migration Expertise**. Do they have the proper skills and talent to mesh your legacy systems with modern digital infrastructure? It is not a rip and replace project. It's more of a migration process.

3. **Proven Relevant Success**. Can they provide proof that they have done this successfully or will you be their first attempt? You will need to see case studies that are similar to your needs and check testimonials. This is a long, challenging, and expensive journey so you want to ensure you work with the right partner who knows your business and industry.

4. **Comprehensive Knowledge and Talent**. Verify that the partner understands best practices in DT and in your industry or business model. You will have your specific systems and needs so you need someone who will understand that and adapt how to best transition into a digital environment.

5. **Solid Support**. When things are wrong and they will, you have to trust in the support to resolve the issues without finger-pointing or some other excuse. If your partner cannot provide the level of support that you need, when you need then it's a no-go out of the gate. Effective communications, people, systems, and processes must be in place to ensure proper support.

HERE IS A SAMPLE CHECKLIST TO HELP YOU IDENTIFY THE BEST PARTNERS FOR YOU.

1. **Location**: Do you have multiple locations in different regions or countries? This will determine if you can go with a local, national, or global partner. Having a local partner support national or international location is probably not feasible. However, having a smaller independent local partner take your business can be more personalized and cost-effective.

2. **Industry**: What type of industry are you in? Is it highly regulated with compliance requirements like Healthcare and Financial? Is it a manufacturer? Is it an SME or enterprise-size? Depending on your answers, you will need to find a partner with the right skills, certifications, credibility, and customer successes. A good rule of thumb is to select a partner who already supports a similar type of business. This is a good indication that they may have the appropriate experience and understands your business enough to better fulfill your needs.

3. **Pick 3**: Most people get quotes from several suppliers whenever they are looking to make a significant purchase. Plan to do the same by interviewing at least 3 partners in each area of need to vent them properly before making

your selection. Compare their skills, apples to apples. Look for important differentiators that matter most to you.

4. **Investigate**: Do your due diligence to ensure they have what you need. Research their websites. Google their name. Talk to their clients. Talk to their staff. Talk to their vendors. Check out their certifications. Look for special awards and recognitions. Check them out on social media networks like LinkedIn, Facebook, and Reddit. Get a good feel for who they are as a company and what their footprint looks like on social media.

5. **Culture**: Look at their management style to gauge if you can get along. Do they project the sort of culture and characteristics that mesh well with your company? If you cannot communicate properly, then things can quickly go bad. Look for an innovative and supportive business culture.

6. **Trust**. Does your "gut" trust them? Were they forthcoming with you? Are they honest? Did you check out their facilities? Are they secure? How long have they been in business? Is their insurance coverage adequate? Talk with their employees!

7. **Technologies**. Most partners can procure just about any solution. In some cases, they will need to be authorized to buy certain brands, but usually, they have ways to work around this hurdle if needed. That said it is always best to stick with partners who are properly authorized and certified to resell the brands of technologies that you need.

8. **Plan**. Where do you want to go and how will you get there from here? What are the outcomes that you want? You need to build a solid roadmap. Start with your destination and work your way back. Include timelines. Always take a phased-in approach by starting to "digitize" the basics and then work your way up. Doing too many things at once can run into snags.

9. **SLA**. Carefully build and review the Service Level Agreement to ensure it meets your standards and requirements. Have your lawyer look it over. Again, every type of business may have a different SLA requirement based on how mission critical the response time is to fix something. This document will govern everything and will be used if any disputes arise.

10. **Monitor**. Never just leave everything up to the partner. It is your business and future so get involved to ensure you are always keeping an eye on your digital transformation progress and outcomes. This can be the most important factor in your future success so live it.

11. **Measure**. Decide how you will measure success and do it regularly. Get the partner to provide periodic reports to outline what they have done and are doing. Measure your internal productivity improvement, talk to your staff for feedback on their performance, check your customer satisfaction levels. Understand if the digital transformation is actually helping your employees, generating more revenue, reducing cost, or improving productivity and customer satisfaction.

12. **Review**. Always keep an eye on your monthly recurring bills. Sometimes you can renegotiate periodically. Look for unused licensing as you increase or decrease your staff. Ensure you are paying only for what you need. Always do a deep review at least once every year where you reserve the right to change the partner, if required.

Demand for DT and talent is already high and with the recent digital-first acceleration, it is growing faster than expected. You may need to pay a premium to hire the best talent. The digital transformation market is estimated to be $336.14 billion in 2020. The managed services market is expected to grow to $257.84 billion by 2022.

A successful digital transformation of your business will become a clear competitive advantage. As such, finding the right partner(s) to help you implement and manage all of your digital IT needs is as mission critical as it gets.

A good analogy for choosing a partner would be to compare to taking a flight. You prefer to have an experienced pilot instead of a rookie. You prefer to fly in a modern plane instead of an older model or one that has a poor track record. Even though the plane has a massive amount of automation and technologies built in and it's generally safe, you still want to have someone with solid experience who you can trust to keep an eye on how the plane is acting and to be ready to take over in case there is an emergency - you want a "SULLY" sitting in the cockpit. You are probably going to want a meticulous pilot who will plan out every step of the flight path to ensure you get to where you want to go with no turbulence, safely and on time.

You expect nothing less from any flight you take so you should seek a similar level of expectations from your DT partner(s). This may not be life or death, but big mistakes from a partner can deeply hurt a company in many ways.

SUMMARY

B y now we are confident that you are 100% aware of the critical importance to digitally reinvent your business and yourself as a leader. We encourage you to keep referring back to our book as a constant source of practical information on how to future-proof your business by embracing the digital-first mindset. Digital reinvention is not a destination. It's also not about technology for the sake of implementing new technology, we are doing it to be customer centric. Fundamentally it's about having the learner's mindset every day as leaders, this mindset must ultimately precipitate into our team, culture, processes and structure to drive real results.

Dr. Denis Cauvier and Shane Gibson deliver customized virtual keynotes, seminars, and workshops on leadership, digital recruitment, social selling, engaging remote workers, and B2B sales. By booking Shane and Denis together as a tandem keynote your audience will get the full benefit of their combined expertise and insights as leading Leadership, Talent Management, Sales, and Marketing thought leaders and authors. You can also of course engage them individually. On the following pages are their bios, contact information.

DR. DENIS CAUVIER
AUTHOR, GLOBAL EXPERT – TALENT MANAGEMENT & LEADERSHIP

D r. Cauvier is an Adjunct Professor at ESC Clermont Graduate School and IPAG University Business School. His leadership and organizational development strategies have added over $850 million in new value/revenue and have boosted his clients' profits by tens of millions of dollars. His clients include hundreds of small/medium companies, family businesses, 200+ multinational firms, dozens of Fortune 500 companies, and several billionaires. With over 30 years as a professional speaker/consultant, Dr. Cauvier has spoken to over 1.7 million people across America and 56 other countries.

Some of Denis' high demand speaking topics include:

- How to capitalize on the global virtual economy.
- How the Digital-First METRICS Model Tool can improve your digital performance.
- How to attract, select, onboard, develop, lead, and engage remote teams.
- How to create a culture that embraces digital transformation

Connect with Denis Cauvier:
Visit: DenisCauvier.com
Connect on LinkedIn: Linkedin.com/in/DrDenisCauvier
Email: Denis@DenisCauvier.com
Or visit realresultsvirtualeconomy.com/connect/ or scan below:

SHANE GIBSON
AUTHOR, SALES THOUGHT LEADER

S hane Gibson is an international speaker and author of four books on sales performance, sales technology, and social selling who has addressed over 200,000 people across five continents. He is #5 on the Forbes.com list of the Top 30 Social Salespeople in the World. He is the founder of the Online Professional Sales Certificate program at Langara College and an accredited training partner of The Canadian Professional Sales Association. His clients include The Ford Motor Company, BMO Financial, Blue Cross, Sun Life, The US Department of Commerce, MicroAge, ChannelNext, The World Brand Congress (India) and dozens of other organizations.

Some of Shane's high demand speaking topics include:

- The 13 big virtual sales trends and how to profit from them.
- The Virtual Sales Professional Competency Map for selecting and developing high-performance digital sales professionals.
- How to build a strong brand in a noisy virtual economy.
- How to leverage social selling to out-sell the competition

Connect with Shane Gibson:
Visit: SalesAcademy.ca
Connect on LinkedIn: Linkedin.com/in/ShaneGibson
Email: Shane@ShaneGibson.com
Or visit realresultsvirtualeconomy.com/connect/ or scan below:

JULIAN LEE
CONTRIBUTING TECHNOLOGY INDUSTRY SUBJECT MATTER EXPERT
FOUNDER OF TECHOPLANET & CHANNELNEXT

Julian Lee has been the president of TechnoPlanet for 30 years. He has witnessed the birth and evolution of the IT Channel (see "About" www.technoplanet.com for milestones). Prior to this and right out of the University of Toronto, he founded a distribution and manufacturing company for Apple third party products that expanded globally.

He is the publisher of eChannelNEWS.com delivering news daily to the channel business community. He is also the organizer of the leading ChannelNEXT technology conferences that educates and brings the IT Industry together several times every year. His core business is helping tech companies to market their products and build channel partner ecosystems.

His most recent mission is to help channel partners to future-proof their businesses through peer-group collaboration (learn more about the resources at www.channelpartneralliance.com). To know what he is currently doing, follow him on LinkedIn www.linkedin.com/in/connectwithjulian.

Scan below to connect with Julian:

BOOK ORDERS

For volume book order quotes and custom branded versions of the book for your organization please visit RealResultsVirtualEconomy.com or scan the code below:

For individual book orders and Kindle versions of the book visit Amazon.com

Manufactured by Amazon.ca
Bolton, ON

37966966R00107